Rona Tutt's Guide to SEND & INCLUSION

Praise for the Book

Rona Tutt's Guide to SEND and Inclusion provides a vital and focused insight into the complex and overlapping worlds of education, politics and academia. By considering inclusion as a process rather than a place, Dr Tutt addresses directly the thorny issue of defining what is meant by the term inclusion and the potential implications for children and young people with SEND.

This book is a useful guide for any educational professionals interested in understanding more about SEND and inclusion, but it is particularly relevant for school leaders, SENCOs and strategic decision makers. Practical activities, case studies and real examples are included throughout to encourage the reader to question and reflect what is happening in their own settings and to consider how they might improve the effectiveness of their own inclusion practices.

In addition to considering the current state of play, Dr Tutt looks back at how attitudes to SEND have changed over time as well as considering what more needs to be done in the future with some attention given to both national and international perspectives.

This book is an essential read and a fantastic opportunity to learn directly from Dr Rona Tutt OBE, one of the leading lights in the world of SEND and inclusion.

Dr Adam Boddison, Chief Executive of nasen
(National Association of Special Educational Needs)

Based on a lifetime of experience in the field, Rona Tutt has written an excellent and engaging introduction to the field of special educational needs/disability and inclusion. The book takes a clear stance about the meaning of inclusion as being about engaging all in education rather than where pupils are placed. She favours a continuum of provision that is used flexibly. She provides a clear summary of the background to the new SEND legislation, its strengths and limitations, while pointing out areas where further improvements can be made. In providing case summaries of different kinds of school provision, this book is a timely introduction to the field for those preparing to become teachers and those about to become SEN coordinators.

Professor Brahm Norwich, University of Exeter

Rona Tutt's Guide to SEND & INCLUSION

Rona Tutt

Los Angeles | London | New Delhi
Singapore | Washington DC | Melbourne

Los Angeles | London | New Delhi
Singapore | Washington DC | Melbourne

SAGE Publications Ltd
1 Oliver's Yard
55 City Road
London EC1Y 1SP

SAGE Publications Inc.
2455 Teller Road
Thousand Oaks, California 91320

SAGE Publications India Pvt Ltd
B 1/I 1 Mohan Cooperative Industrial Area
Mathura Road
New Delhi 110 044

SAGE Publications Asia-Pacific Pte Ltd
3 Church Street
#10-04 Samsung Hub
Singapore 049483

Editor: Jude Bowen
Assistant editor: George Knowles
Production editor: Nicola Marshall
Project manager: Jeanette Graham
Copyeditor: Rosemary Campbell
Proofreader: Sharon Cawood
Indexer: Rona Tutt
Marketing manager: Dilhara Attygalle
Cover design: Wendy Scott
Typeset by: C&M Digitals (P) Ltd, Chennai, India
Printed and bound by CPI Group (UK) Ltd,
Croydon, CR0 4YY

Library of Congress Control Number: 2016935503

British Library Cataloguing in Publication data

A catalogue record for this book is available from
the British Library

ISBN 9781473954793
ISBN 9781473954809 (pbk)

At SAGE we take sustainability seriously. Most of our products are printed in the UK using FSC papers and boards.
When we print overseas we ensure sustainable papers are used as measured by the PREPS grading system.
We undertake an annual audit to monitor our sustainability.

I would like to dedicate this book, firstly to the children and young people who need our understanding, and, secondly, to those who try to provide the support they deserve.

Contents

About the author

 **Dr Rona Tutt OBE** has taught pupils of all ages in state and independent, day and residential, mainstream and special schools. She has been a winner of the Leadership in Teaching Award, received an Outstanding Reviewer Award for her work on the *International Journal of Educational Management* and an OBE for her services to special needs education. She is a Past President of the National Association of Head Teachers (NAHT) and continues to be involved in their work, particularly in the field of SEND.

Since moving on from headship, Rona has been in constant demand as a speaker, reviewer, writer and judge. She has been part of the Expert Reference Group of the Autism Education Trust (AET) since its inception and was the Interim Chair of Hertfordshire's All-Age Autism Partnership Board from April 2015 to March 2016. In the same year, she was asked to be on the Strategic Advisory Group for 'KIDS', a charity for disabled young people and their families, and to be their writer for the DfE- funded project *Making it Personal*, which is known as MIP3. She represents NAHT on the Special Education Consortium (SEC) (an umbrella group for over 30 organisations involved in SEN & disability); the Joint Unions Group on SEN Issues; and the National SEND Forum (NSENDF).

Rona is vice chair of governors at two schools: one is a secondary school for pupils who have moderate learning difficulties (MLD), autism, and speech, language and communication needs (SLCN); the other is an all-age school for profoundly deaf pupils, where many pupils have British Sign Language (BSL) as their first language rather than English. Having trained originally as a Teacher of the Deaf, Rona is working through her exams in BSL and learning about deaf culture.

Rona is the author of: *Every Child Included*, (2007); she co-authored *Educating Children with Complex Conditions – Understanding Overlapping and Co-existing Developmental Disorders* (Dittrich and Tutt 2008); wrote *Partnership Working to Support Special Educational Needs and Disabilities* in 2010; co-authored *How Successful Schools Work – The Impact of Innovative School Leadership* (Tutt and Williams 2012) and *The SEND Code of Practice: 0–25 years* (Tutt and Williams 2015).

Acknowledgements

I would like to thank all the very many colleagues, friends and families who, over the years, have contributed to my thinking about how best to ensure that children and young people who have special educational needs and/or disability receive the most appropriate and effective education.

In addition, I would like to acknowledge the help given to me in writing this book by those who have contributed directly to it. Some of them are named in this book, but many others are not. They include people who allowed me to visit and others who gave up their time to talk to me. They include:

John Ayres	Principal, Grangewood School & CEO of The Eden Academy
Moira Banks	School Improvement Officer Inclusion, N. Tyneside Council
David Bateson	Chair, National SEND Forum (NSENDF)
Chris Britten	Head teacher, Ysgol Y Deri, Wales
Robert Campbell	Principal, Impington Village College
Barry Carpenter	Honorary Professor at the Universities of Worcester, Limerick, Hamburg and Flinders, Australia
Raymond Cassidy	Principal, Rathore School, Northern Ireland
Andrew Clark	School Improvement Adviser, Hertfordshire
Dawn Copping	Head teacher, Shaw Primary Academy
John Cregg	Head teacher, Priestnall School
Graeme Daniel	President of the Special Education Principals' Association of New Zealand (SPANZ)
Colm Davis	Chair, Strategic Leadership Forum for Special Schools in NI
Claire Dorer	Chief Executive of the National Association of Special Schools (NASS)
Niki Elliot	Principal Lecturer at Sheffield Hallam University and Chair of the Special Education Consortium (SEC)

Sandra Flynn	Principal, Lisanally School, Northern Ireland
Corina Foster	Head teacher, The Valley School
Melanie Foster	Group Manager SEN and Inclusion, Newham
Jo Galloway	Head teacher, Radlett Lodge
Rob Gasson	CEO and Executive Principal, Acorn Academy
Sharon Gray	UK Hub Director for ecl Foundation (enhancing children's lives) and Director, Wholehearted Learning
David Harrison	Former head teacher
James Hourigan	Strategic Lead for SEN Reform, Newham
Peter Imray	SEN Training and Advice
Clare Jones	Head teacher, Bignold Primary School and Nursery
Paula Jordan	Principal, Sperrinview School, Northern Ireland
Simon Knight	Deputy Head, Frank Wise School
Edel Lavery	Principal, Donard School, Northern Ireland
Howard Lay	Chief Executive, Samuel Ward Academy Trust
Jon Lees	Specialist Education Services (SES)
Steve Lord	Specialist Education Services (SES)
Judge Jane McConnell	SEND Tribunal
Marijka Miles	Head teacher, Prospect School
Jacki Mitchell	Head teacher, Woodston School
Gareth Morewood	SENCO and Head of Curriculum Support, Priestnall School
Tony Newman	Former head teacher, Stanley School
Dave Nutting	National Network of Parent Carer Forums
Lorraine Petersen	Former chief executive of nasen
Helen Plank	National Network of Parent Carer Forums
Barbara Slider	Head teacher, Shiremoor Primary School and head of Shine Teaching School Alliance
Lynn Slinger	Forest Way Teaching School Alliance
Dame Dela Smith	Founder of the Darlington Education Village
June Venus	Principal, Yanwath Primary School

Sarah Wild	Head teacher, Limpsfield Grange School
Rob Williams	Policy Director, NAHT Cymru
Louise Casey	
Katie Fraser	
Helen Holford	
Caroline Jenkin	
Richard Weinbaum	

Delegates to the Shine SEND Conference 2015

And to Tricia Murphy, former President of nasen, who allowed me to run my thoughts past her, while we were supposed to be relaxing at a spa.

Finally, my thanks to Jude Bowen, Amy Jarrold and George Knowles at SAGE, for their support, encouragement, good humour and patience.

Abbreviations and acronyms

AAC   Augmentative and alternative communication

ADHD   Attention deficit hyperactivity disorder

AFA   Achievement for All

AHDS   Association of Headteachers and Deputes in Scotland

ALN   Additional learning needs

AP   Alternative provision

APPG   All-Party Parliamentary Group

ARP   Additionally resourced provision

ASD   Autistic spectrum disorder

ASN   Additional Support Needs

BACP   British Association of Counselling and Psychotherapists

BESD   Behaviour, emotional and social development

BSL   British sign language

CAMHS   Child and adolescent mental health services

CCG   Clinical Commissioning Group

CEO   Chief education officer

CHES   Community and Hospital Education Service

CPD   Continuing professional development

DCO   Designated Clinical Officer

DMO   Designated Medical Officer

DVT   Driver Youth Trust charity

EAL   English as an additional language

ECM   Every Child Matters

EHC plan   Education, Health and Care plan

EiC   Excellence in Cities

ELSA   Emotional literacy support assistant

EP	Educational psychologist
EPicc	Extended provision for the inclusion of challenging children
EPS	Educational psychology service
ERA	Education Reform Act
ESBD	Emotional, social and behavioural difficulties
EWS	Education welfare service
FAS	Foetal alcohol syndrome
FASD	Foetal alcohol spectrum disorder
FE	Further education
FSM	Free school meals
HE	Higher education
IB	International Baccalaureate
ILC	Interactive learning centre
IQM	Inclusion Quality Mark
ITT	Initial teacher training
KS	Key stage
LA	Local authority
LAC	Looked after children
LD	Learning difficulties
LDA	Learning difficulty assessment
LDD	Learning difficulties and disabilities
LEA	Local Education Authority
LLE	Local leader of education
LSA	Learning support assistant
MAT	Multi-academy trust
MITA	Maximising the Impact of Teaching Assistants
MLD	Moderate learning difficulties
MSA	Midday supervisory assistant
NAS	National Autistic Society
NASS	National Association of Non-Maintained Special Schools
nasen	National Association for Special Educational Needs

NATSPEC   The Association of National Specialist Colleges

NCTL   National College for Teaching and Leadership

NEET   Not in education, employment or training

NHS   National Health Service

NI   Northern Ireland

NLE   National leader of education

NLG   National leader of governance

NMSS   Non-maintained special school

NSN   New Schools Network

NSS   National support school

Ofsted   Office for Standards in Education

OT   Occupational therapist

PD   Physical disabilities

PDA   Pathological demand avoidance (syndrome)

PEP   Personal education plan

PMLD   Profound and multiple learning difficulties

PRU   Pupil referral unit

PSHCE   Personal, social, health and citizenship education

PSHE   Personal, social and health education

QTS   Qualified teacher status

RNIB   Royal National Institute of Blind People

RSC   Regional Schools Commissioner

SAT   Single academy trust

SEAL   Social and emotional aspects of learning

SEBD   Social, emotional and behavioural difficulties

SEMH   Social, emotional and mental health difficulties

SEND   Special educational needs and disability

SENDA   Special Educational Needs and Disability Act

SEPANZ   Special Education Principals Association of New Zealand

SES   Specialist Education Services

SLCN   Speech, language and communication needs

SLD	Severe learning difficulties
SLE	Specialist leader of education
SLT	Senior leadership team
SPD	Sensory processing disorder
SWAT	Samuel Ward Academy Trust
TES	Times Educational Supplement
UK	United Kingdom
UN	United Nations
UNCRC	UN Convention on the Rights of the Child
UNESCO	UN Educational, Scientific and Cultural Organization
WHO	World Health Organization

How to use this book

After a lifetime of working in the field of SEN and disability I had mixed feelings about writing this book. On the one hand, it was the one book I most wanted to write. On the other hand, I did not wish to return to the contentious discussions about what inclusion means in the context of children and young people who have special educational needs and/or disability (SEND). However, the need to add any weight I had to bringing to an end the use of the word 'inclusion' as a shorthand for every child being educated in their local school, became the overriding one.

The argument for seeing inclusion as involving a flexible continuum of provision, within which every child and every educational setting can be included, is developed throughout the chapters. However, some readers may prefer to alight first on the one that catches their interest. Unlike a novel, readers have the flexibility to decide their own route.

The Introduction provides a brief overview of how attitudes towards disability have changed over the years, which leads into the debate that dominated the 1980s and 1990s about the right of special schools to exist. It touches on the international dimension and the various models of disability.

The remaining chapters have a similar format:

- an overview of what is covered in the chapter at the start
- 'Key information' highlighted throughout
- 'Questions for reflection' and 'Activities' are factored in at relevant points to encourage readers to interact with the text and to provide ideas for wider discussion and debate
- a summary at the end
- suggestions for further reading.

In addition, Chapters 2–6 feature case studies of schools, settings and services, which serve to illustrate the innovative practice that exists throughout the continuum of provision.

Chapter 1 covers the SEND Reforms that were implemented from September 2014, although embedding the change of culture they represent is expected to take many years. After a brief synopsis of how the changes came about and what they were trying to achieve, there is a critical look at how far they have been successful and what more might have been achieved as part of this major overhaul of the special needs system.

Chapter 2 explains why there is a much more complex and vulnerable population of pupils entering the school system. This being so, the case is made for the need for more specialist provision in all its forms, rather than talking about reducing the number of special schools and other forms of specialist and alternative provision.

Chapter 3 looks at how mainstream and special schools, as well as alternative provision, have all had to adapt to meet the needs of children and young people in today's educational settings. It considers what parents look for and goes on to discuss ways in which bullying and exclusions can be reduced by making sure those with SEND receive the right sort of provision.

Chapter 4 considers how, once a continuum of provision is in place, it needs to be used flexibly, both to support the changing needs of individuals and the requirements of a changing population as a whole. It suggests that this is achieved through schools, services and other settings working together in various partnerships and collaborations.

Chapter 5 concentrates more specifically on how to meet the different needs mentioned in the 2015 SEND Code of Practice, with additional sections on autism, behaviour and mental health issues. The chapter also looks at measuring the progress of pupils with SEND and at what is happening to improve trainee teachers' understanding of these children and young people.

Chapter 6 features case studies of two different local authorities, in terms of how they provide a flexible continuum of provision. It also looks at the SEN system in New Zealand, before reiterating the need to come to a common understanding of what inclusion means in the context of children and young people who have SEND.

The **concluding chapter** moves on from what is happening currently to look at what more needs to be done. It suggests a series of steps that need to be taken in order to ensure that there is a common understanding of how to move forward in a way that will improve outcomes for children and young people, as well as improving the quality of their educational experiences.

Introduction: Changing attitudes to SEND

'I want to be where I feel I belong.'

Chapter overview

This introductory chapter explains what lies at the heart of this book, namely the need to agree on what is meant by inclusion, in order to move forward with a united view. It explains how:

- Attitudes to people with disabilities have changed over time
- National and international legislation has influenced people's opinions of those who are disabled
- Models of disability have changed along with these changing attitudes.

The chapter ends with a preliminary discussion about the meaning of inclusion in the context of pupils who have SEND, a theme which is developed further throughout this book.

Changing attitudes

For too long, the inclusion of children and young people who have special educational needs and/or disabilities (SEND) has been held back by a failure to agree on what inclusion in this context really means. The first part of this chapter considers how attitudes have changed from an almost total lack of understanding about people who are disabled to one where considerable efforts have been made to meet their needs, although much more remains to be done. These changes are traced through the terminology that has been used and through different models of disability. An increased understanding has led to a number of legislative changes, both in the UK and internationally.

The 18th and 19th centuries

In the 1760s, Thomas Braidwood founded schools for deaf children in Edinburgh and London, while the same decade saw the founding of schools for the visually impaired in Edinburgh and Bristol. Schools for those with sensory impairments opened up new opportunities for pupils to communicate through sign language or through Braille. By the 19th century, other types of special schools were beginning to emerge, including The Cripples and Industrial School for Girls in London, where pupils were given lessons in reading and writing, as well as training in straw plaiting, straw hat making and needlework, and the St Martin's Home for Crippled Boys, which taught trades such as tailoring and boot-making. The latter was founded by the Waifs and Strays Society, which is known today as the Children's Society. Local authorities (LAs) were made responsible for providing education to blind and deaf children from 1893.

The first half of the 20th century

The 1918 Education Act made schooling compulsory for all disabled children, and by 1921, there were more than 300 institutions for blind, deaf, crippled, tubercular and epileptic children. Despite these developments, a stark reminder of attitudes at this time is reflected in the way the royal family responded to the arrival of Prince John. Born in 1905, he was the sixth and youngest child of King George V and Queen Mary. It is thought John was severely epileptic and may have had other difficulties as well. Whatever the extent of his medical problems, he was seen as 'not quite right', and so he was kept from public view. From 1916 until his death three years later, he lived in a cottage on the Sandringham estate with his nurse and a male orderly. Although this might be seen today as an uncaring attitude, it was very much in keeping with the times and it did enable Prince John to avoid the normal pressures of royal life. He died suddenly in his sleep aged 13 in January 1919. What does seem shocking in today's climate is a letter Prince Edward (later Edward VIII) wrote to his lover, Freda Dudley Ward, on learning that Prince John had died:

> ... His death is the greatest relief imaginable & what we've always silently prayed for. ... No one would be more cut up if any of my other 3 brothers were to die than I should be, but this poor boy had become more of an animal than anything else & was only a brother in the flesh & nothing else. (Quoted in Greig 2011, *The King Maker: The Man Who Saved George VI*).

This attitude of 'out sight, out of mind' continued, and in the 1930s young people with disabilities continued to be shut away from their families and local communities. However, places like the pioneering community of Sunfield developed a more holistic approach to the care and education of disabled children. Barry Carpenter, who was its chief executive for many years, explains that, although Sunfield had started at a time when families wanted their 'handicapped' children shut away, the school turned this round to the point where he could say: 'We do not take in children; we welcome families as part of our community' (quoted in Tutt 2007: 87).

Before the 1944 Act, which was mainly concerned with providing universal free education at secondary level, the education of handicapped children had been considered separately, but from this time, they became the responsibility of Local Education Authorities (LEAs), who had to make sure these children were seen by a medical officer, to determine whether the child was 'suffering from any disability of mind or body and as to the nature and extent of any such disability'. The Act established 11 categories of disability. As well as physical handicap and sensory impairments (blind and partially sighted; deaf and partially deaf), the list included: delicate, diabetic and epileptic; speech defect, maladjusted and educationally subnormal.

Despite the problems caused by the war, after the 1944 Act, special education provision improved. Although far too late to help Prince John, methods of controlling epilepsy had moved forward and teachers in mainstream schools were increasingly willing to accept responsibility for less severe cases if they had medical support. The number of special schools rose substantially, including 25 new boarding schools for children with physical handicaps, such as cerebral palsy, and open air schools for delicate children. The development of provision for children with speech defects was delayed, but the number of speech therapists employed by LEAs increased.

The second half of the 20th century

A major shift in attitude was the 1970 Education (Handicapped Children) Act, which brought all children into education and stopped classifying some of them as uneducable on the grounds that they were 'suffering from a disability of mind'. This meant that all those who had been under the care of the health authorities became the responsibility of the LEAs.

Not long after this, the Warnock Report of 1978 and the 1981 Education Act that followed it, set off a lengthy and divisive debate about the role of special schools. The Warnock Committee's use of the phrase 'special educational needs' (SEN) was admirable in its desire to move away from placing children in categories of need rather than treating them as individuals. The downside was that it led some people to forget the very real difference between educating those with very significant needs and the majority of pupils with SEND who have always been in mainstream education. In a pamphlet Warnock wrote in 2005 (Warnock 2005: 13), she recognised that the umbrella term, 'SEN', had had its problems: 'Not only is there a gradation of needs which our early thinking did not adequately address, there is also a wide range of different kinds of need'. In the pamphlet and since writing it, she has spoken many times of her wish for special schools to be part of the provision available for pupils with special needs.

During the 1980s 'integration' was a buzzword, with the idea that an increasing number of individuals should be integrated into mainstream education. In the 1990s, this changed to 'inclusion', which suggested that schools themselves should change to accommodate all the pupils who wanted to come to them. These two decades were a time when special schools took a battering, as the media and others jumped on the bandwagon of inclusion being interpreted as *every* child being in a mainstream school. The effect was that, after years of development, special schools began to decrease in number. The 1988 Education Reform Act (ERA) introduced a national curriculum, which all children, whether in mainstream or special education, had to follow, and schools for pupils with severe learning difficulties (SLD), and profound and multiple learning difficulties (PMLD) in particular, went to great lengths to try to balance what was appropriate for their pupils with what they were required to do.

In 1994 the first Code of Practice on identifying and assessing special needs for all schools was published.

A new century and a more pragmatic approach

Although opinion remained divided about the place of special schools, by the turn of the century a rather more pragmatic approach had begun to creep in, as the reality of trying to meet an increasingly wide range of needs in mainstream schools began to come into conflict with successive governments' fixation on a 'standards agenda', whereby schools are expected to show an increase in academic results year on year. The role played by Ofsted (the school's inspection service) in judging schools by a narrow range of academic results exacerbated the gulf between these two agendas.

The first sign that times were changing in terms of the place of special schools, came when the then Labour government established a working party to look at the future of special schools. The findings fed into the government's SEN strategy, *Removing Barriers to Achievement* (DfES 2004a). On the one hand, this gave a continuing role to special schools, but, on the other, it suggested that numbers in them would continue to fall as mainstream teachers became more skilled at meeting a wider range of needs. The role for special schools was seen as a dual one: educating those with the most complex needs and supporting mainstream schools in acquiring further expertise.

In 2005–06, the Education Select Committee held an Inquiry into SEN and asked Andrew Adonis, Minister for SEN at the time, to clarify the government's position on inclusion. Lord Adonis replied that, rather than continuing to talk about inclusion, the government would prefer to emphasise the need to have 'a flexible continuum of provision'. He agreed that an overhaul of the SEN system was needed and suggested it might happen in a few years' time. (More recent history around the SEND Reforms is covered in the next chapter).

Questions for reflection

A former secretary of state for education, David Blunkett, who, having been blind since birth, carried out his role with the aid of guide dogs, has said: 'Progress in school learning is ultimately about the quality of life post-school.'
　　Think about:

1.　Whether you agree with this statement
2.　What it might mean in terms of some of the children and young people you know or have worked with, who have a range of different needs.

The international dimension to inclusion

In 1990, the UK signed the UN Convention on the Rights of the Child (UNCRC) and ratified it in 1991. The Convention stresses the right of all children to be educated and to have their views listened to. It also states that a mentally or physically disabled child should enjoy a full and decent life. More recently, when introducing the Children and Families Bill, the Coalition Government reminded LAs to have regard to UNCRC and to ensure that children and young people were involved in the development of local services.

In 1994, in common with most other countries, the UK government supported what became known as the Salamanca Statement. This came out of a World Conference on SEN, which was organised by UNESCO and attended by the governments of 92 countries. This set out that those with SEN must have access to regular schools. The statement went on to recognise that countries were at different points, with some (such as the UK), having well-established systems of special schools for specific types of need. These are described as representing a valuable resource for other schools, so that special schools or units within mainstream schools may provide the most suitable education for a relatively small number of children with disabilities whose needs cannot be met in regular class-rooms or schools.

Meanwhile, in the UK the term SEN, which comes from education, and disability, which comes from health, were brought together in the Special Educational Needs and Disability Act 2001. Under the Act, schools were prohibited from discriminating against disabled children and were required to make reasonable adjustments to include them. The Act strengthened the right to a mainstream education for children with SEN by making it clear that if parents wanted a mainstream education for their child every-thing possible should be done to provide it. Equally, where parents wanted a special school place, their wishes should be taken into account.

In 2006, the UN Convention on the Rights of Persons with Disabilities (UNCRPD) was adopted by the UN General Assembly. This helped to change attitudes from seeing disabled people as objects of charity, to subjects with rights to make decisions about their own lives and become active members of society. Article 24 of UNCRPD guarantees all disabled learners the right to be part of the general education system. In ratifying the Convention, the UK Government explained that its interpretation of 'general education' included both mainstream and special schools and that parents should continue to have access to places in either type of school.

In 2010, the Equality Act provided a legal framework for protection against discrimination on the grounds of nine 'protected characteristics', namely:

- Age
- Disability
- Gender reassignment
- Marriage and civil partnership
- Pregnancy and maternity
- Race
- Religion or belief
- Sex
- Sexual orientation.

Key information: The rights of disabled people

International

1990 The UN Convention on the Rights of the Child (UNCRC) was signed by the UK in 1991.

1994 UNESCO's *Salamanca Statement* supported pupils with SEN having access to regular schools, while seeing a dual role for special schools.

2006 The UN Convention on the Rights of Persons with Disabilities (UNCRPD) was adopted by the UN General Assembly.

UK

2001 The Special Educational Needs and Disability Act (SENDA) brought the two terms together.

2010 The Equality Act brought together previous pieces of legislation and specified the groups that should be protected.

Differences across the UK

As Hodkinson (2015) points out, within the United Kingdom the educational provision for children with learning difficulties operates differently under the various legislative systems. Scotland has always been further apart from England in terms of its education system. In 2004, an Education Act abolished the term 'SEN' and replaced it with 'Additional Support Needs' (ASN). This refers to any child or young person who would benefit from extra help in order to overcome barriers to their learning. In 2005, Northern Ireland (NI) increased the rights of children with SEN to attend mainstream schools and introduced disability discrimination laws for the whole of the education system. Wales had, until now, retained the use of the term 'SEN' alongside its own SEN Code of Practice. However, a Draft Additional Learning Needs Bill (Wales) has suggested replacing SEN with Additional Learning Needs (ALN) and a Draft Additional Learning Needs Code has been issued. Although the new term would encompass both those currently described as having SEN and those who, at post-16, have been described as having Learning Difficulties and Disabilities (LDD), it does not go beyond this to take in other vulnerable groups.

Models of disability

Earlier in this chapter, there was a reference to the medical model of disability, which held sway before the social model of disability suggested an alternative viewpoint. More recently, a third model has been suggested, which incorporates elements from both the medical and the social models.

The medical model

The medical model arose from the way the 1944 Education Act, mentioned earlier, categorised children. Decisions about where these young learners were educated was often determined largely by the category they were placed in, rather than their ability to benefit from a mainstream curriculum. This model sees disability solely as a medical condition, and any difficulties that are encountered lie within the disabled person, rather than being affected by the environment within which they operate. The medical profession is seen as trying to cure or improve the disability and it is doctors who decide the disabled person's right to have financial assistance or healthcare support.

The social model

In the 1970s, another model of disability began to be developed, which was in direct opposition to the medical model and seen by many to be a more inclusive approach. The social model of disability draws on the idea that it is society that disables people through designing everything to meet the needs of the majority of people who are not disabled. There is a recognition within the social model that there is a great deal society can do to reduce, and ultimately remove, some of these disabling barriers, and that this task is the responsibility of society as a whole, rather than the disabled person.

Towards an interactionist model

A model which combines features of both these two models has been recognised by the World Health Organization (WHO). This model of disability involves a consideration of the interaction between features of a person's body and features of the society in which that person lives. Back in 1981, Klaus Weddell took this approach when working on the 1981 Education Act. In 2002, Tom Shakespeare, whose achondroplasia gives him a particular insight into models of disability, and his co-author, Nicholas Watson, wrote a paper arguing that the time had come to move on from the social model of disability. They argued that the way it has been characterised in the UK meant it had outlived its usefulness and had led to a position being taken beyond just the need to remove barriers – which they agree is correct – and leading in some cases to opposition to medical interventions that might help the disabled person. They write:

> People are disabled both by social barriers and by their bodies. This is straightforward and uncontroversial. The British social model approach, because it 'over-eggs the pudding', risks discrediting the entire dish. (Shakespeare and Watson 2002: 15)

Key information: Models of disability

The two best-known models are:

1. **The medical model** which sees the difficulty as residing within the person who has the disability. This is sometimes referred to as the 'deficit model'.

2. **The social model** which sees any difficulty as a result of the society in which the disabled person lives, and the inability of that society to adapt to the needs of people who are disabled.

More recently, there have been attempts to marry these two approaches by designing an *interactionist model*, which recognises both factors within the child *and* the context in which a person lives.

Inclusion as a process not a place

In a discussion paper written in 2015, Nick Peacey refers to Brahm Norwich (2013), pointing out that the word 'inclusion' is typically used in two senses:

- The process of implementing the rights of *all* liable to exclusion to full participation in education or society
- Increasing the placement of learners in mainstream education.

While there may be differences of opinion as to how the first bullet point can be best achieved, most would agree that it should happen. It is the second bullet point that sums up the debate that raged throughout the 1980s and 1990s and has never entirely gone away. Lorraine Petersen, who spent ten years as chief executive of nasen – the largest organisation for SEND in the country – says that her interpretation of inclusion is one where:

The child or young person receives an education that best suits their needs at any particular time. It does not mean that everyone has to be in the same building, but that there is the staffing and the resources to meet their needs.

The rest of the chapters in this book build on the idea that inclusion is a process by which children and young people can be properly included in education, so that they are prepared for life beyond school, whatever form that might take. In order to achieve this and to meet the needs of an increasingly complex population of young learners, there has to be a broad continuum of provision, so that every child and young person can be included in a meaningful sense in education. Special schools should never be seen as the last resort when all else fails, but as the very best option for the small percentage of children who need them. Equality is not about giving everyone the same experiences, but about recognising that, while everyone is different, they should be equally valued and educated in an environment where they feel they belong.

Summary

This introductory chapter has looked at how people's attitudes towards those who have SEND have changed from an uncaring one to one recognising their inalienable right to be included in education and in society. Points of disagreement were rehearsed about the nature of disability and the meaning of inclusion itself.

The chapter ended with a brief introduction to the central theme of the book, that of the need for agreement about inclusion being a process not a place and that a broad continuum of provision has the best chance of giving every young learner an education that will prepare them for life in the wider world.

Further reading

Hodkinson A. (2015) *Key Issues in Special Educational Needs and Inclusion*, 2nd edition. London: Sage.

Peacey, N. (2015) 'A transformation or an opportunity lost?' A discussion paper prepared for Research and Information on State Education (RISE). www.risetrust.org.uk

Shakespeare, T. and Watson, N. (2002) 'The social model of disability: an outdated ideology?' *Research in Social Science and Disability* 2: 9–28.

Tutt, R. (2007) *Every Child Included*. London: Sage.

1

The benefits, drawbacks and omissions of the SEND Reforms

'I am the expert on my own child.'

Chapter overview

The SEND Reforms which formed Part Three of the Children and Families Act 2014 were described as the biggest shake up of the system for over 30 years. As the changes are in the throes of being embedded, this chapter considers:

- The background to the reforms
- The main changes and what they were designed to achieve
- The benefits and drawbacks of the reforms
- The opportunities that were missed.

The chapter ends with an explanation of why the changes to the SEND system were important in terms of an opportunity to agree on the meaning of inclusion.

The SEND Reforms

Although there had been some tweaking of the SEN system introduced by the Warnock Committee in 1978 and consolidated by the 1981 Education Act, there had been no attempt at a major overhaul until the Coalition Government decided to implement the major review that had been called for as an outcome of the Education Select Committee's Inquiry into SEN (mentioned in the previous chapter).

The lead up to the Reforms

In September 2010, Ofsted published a survey report: *The Special Educational Needs and Disability Review*. The aim of the review was to evaluate how well the SEN system was working currently, rather than suggesting how it might be improved. The report stated that, at that time, one in five pupils were seen as having SEN, with those who had statements remaining fairly constant at around 2.8%, while those with non-statemented SEN had risen from 14% to 18.2%. The report argued that as many as half those placed on School Action 'would not be identified as having special educational needs if schools focused on improving teaching and learning for all, with individual goals for improvement'. With the removal of School Action and School Action Plus, the figure for non-statemented SEN pupils decreased.

In a previous report, *Inclusion: Does It Matter Where Children Are Taught?* (2006), Ofsted had argued that the most effective setting was specialist provision attached to a mainstream school. In the 2010 report, there was an interesting shift (perhaps in keeping with the general move to be more pragmatic and less dogmatic), as this time the inspectors stated that: 'No one model – such as special schools, full inclusion in mainstream settings, or specialist units co-located with mainstream settings – worked better than any other' (Ofsted 2010: 7). Instead, the key was said to be that, wherever pupils were taught, there was a focus on good quality teaching and learning, close tracking, rigorous monitoring of progress and evaluating the impact of any interventions.

Shortly after Ofsted's report was published, Sarah Teather, who was the Minister with responsibility for SEN at the time, published the *Green Paper: Children and Young People with Special Educational Needs and Disabilities – Call for Views* (DfE 2010b), which invited people to respond with their ideas on how the SEN system might be improved. Teather received many thousands of comments from parents and professionals who queued up to tell her what was wrong with the system at the time, rather than telling her how it might be improved. A few months later, in March 2011, *Support and Aspiration: A New Approach to SEND – a Consultation* was published, setting out some of the government's thinking. This accepted Ofsted's view about the over-identification of SEN. The main changes that were proposed were piloted by some SEND Pathfinder Local Authorities (LAs) working with their partners in the health service.

The main changes

The main changes became Part Three of the Children and Families Act 2014. In essence, they can be summarised as follows:

- Placing the aspirations, interests and wishes of parents and children at the centre and engaging them in the decision-making process
- Extending SEND to cover 0–25 years and preparing for adulthood from the earliest years
- Co-ordinating assessments that may lead to an Education, Health and Care plan (EHC plan) (these replace statements)
- Services commissioning jointly the support the child or young person needs
- Parents being offered a personal budget, if requested, as part of an EHC plan
- LAs to be responsible for producing a Local Offer, giving all the information about the support and activities available in their area
- Developing the workforce so that they understand person-centred planning
- Every teacher being seen as a teacher of pupils with SEND, while special educational needs co-ordinators (SENCOs) take a more strategic role
- SEN Support to replace the two categories of School Action and School Action Plus.

What the changes were designed to achieve

At the centre of these changes lies a change in culture, whereby children, young people and their families, are placed at the heart of making the decisions that affect them, rather than the professionals around them deciding what should happen. For some schools and other settings, which have always treated parents as partners and where the voice of the child is prominent, little change may have been necessary. For others, this provided an opportunity to consider ways of working even more closely with families, so that they are not just kept informed, but fully involved in the decisions that are made about their child. This applies to pupils on SEN Support as well as those with an EHC plan. The emphasis in the SEND Code of Practice 2015 is on all teachers, whether class or subject teachers, taking responsibility for the progress of all the pupils they teach, rather than relying on the SENCO, who takes on a more strategic role. The move from having two categories of need for those without EHC plans to the one category of SEN Support, has resulted in a reduction in this group of pupils, although the reasons for this are not entirely clear.

Questions for reflection

'I talked of the home-school relationship. I talked of my expertise, as the parent of a child with an at-birth diagnosis – I reminded them that the biggest expert in my child was me, not them.'

Think about the above statement by a parent of a child with Down's syndrome and about why she may have felt the staff needed reminding of her role as her child's main carer.

Reflect on the parents and carers you have known, or may be in contact with now, and what more you might have done to establish a more equal partnership.

Benefits and drawbacks of the SEND Reforms

The move to parents and professionals working in partnership, rather than the professionals being the ones to take the lead, is becoming common across services and has been generally welcomed in the context of the SEND Reforms. Writing in the SEN Magazine for November 2015, Elizabeth Stanley, Director of 'Wraparound Partnership' (www.wraparoundpartnership.org), put it this way:

> The previous system of statementing, School Action and School Action Plus was very much process driven and became, in the end, about jumping through hoops in order to access provision, rather than talking about aspirations and how to make these a reality. (Stanley 2015, *Power to Parents*)

So, now there is the opportunity to take the family's aspirations as the starting point, and, while taking account of the child's needs, to think about the outcomes that will result in those aspirations and the provision needed to achieve them:

Aspirations $\longrightarrow$ Needs $\longrightarrow$ Provision $\longrightarrow$ Outcomes

Several families have said how they prefer having a more positive way of thinking about the future, and, whether or not they are in receipt of an EHC plan, having a chance to say what their child can do, as well as describing his or her difficulties.

0–25

One of the changes that has been welcomed as a very positive move is the extension of the age range to cover 0 to 25 years. Parents are now able to have an assessment and the possibility of an EHC plan before their child starts formal education. This has the potential of making both early identification and early intervention more of a reality. At the other end of the age range, the extension up to 25 years recognises that children with learning difficulties of all kinds may need support for longer, and it has the added benefit of making it easier to transfer from children's to adult services in a more seamless way. Both should help young people with SEND to have longer to develop their skills and increase their independence.

Assessments and EHC plans

As with the process of getting a statement, an assessment may or may not lead to the production of an EHC plan. If a parent is concerned about their child's progress, they can submit a request to the LA for an EHC needs assessment to be carried out. Schools may also make the request for a pupil to be assessed. While the process may sound very similar to the evidence-gathering for a statement, where it differs is in making sure that the views, aspirations and feelings of children, young people and their families are very much part of the whole process. There is evidence to suggest that many parents have enjoyed a more personal approach being taken and have appreciated the move to person-centred planning. It has made them feel that their voices are heard, their opinions matter and they are not detached from making the decisions that affect them. To date, there would seem to be less evidence that young people have felt more involved.

Many EHC plans are much more personal and reflect the individual child rather than being written in the more formal language used for statements. Some LA officers who have written statements in the past without ever meeting the family concerned have said that they have enjoyed being re-trained to work face to face with the families. The downside is that giving time for children, young people and their families to feel fully involved in the process has meant that EHC plans take longer to produce than statements. LAs have found it difficult to keep up with implementing new assessments while also in the process of transferring thousands of existing statements to EHC plans. Although they have been given from September 2014 to 1 April 2018 to cover the transition, this has meant a considerable increase in workload. So far, few parents have taken up the option of a personal budget, which is a new concept in education, although interest may increase over time. However, there are two factors which may have contributed to this not being a popular option: firstly, parents have to know they can request that a personal budget is prepared alongside the EHC plan; secondly, although LAs must consider such a request, there are circumstances in which they do not have to agree to go ahead.

Joint working and commissioning

Since the 2004 Children Act, education and social care have worked more closely together, often under the same director, but, on the ground, professionals from the different services may have a limited contact with, or understanding of, each other's roles and perspectives. Yet, young learners who have SEND may need to draw on all three services. It would be a significant step forward if health could join education and social care in a single structure, but a lack of coterminous boundaries can be another difficulty, as well as the reorganisations that go on within the health service.

The SEND Code of Practice 2015 has made further strides in trying to bring the services closer together, through the role of a Designated Medical Officer (DMO) or a Designated Clinical Officer (DCO), who supports relationships across the health sector and between education, health and care partners. It is common for one DMO/DCO to cover a number of Clinical Commissioning Group (CCG) areas. While services need to commission support jointly and address children's needs in a more holistic way, the same difficulties that existed with statements remain, i.e. getting services that are short staffed and strapped for cash to work together and to make young learners with SEND a priority. Health services, for instance, may be more concerned with finding enough money to meet the medical needs of an ageing population.

The Reforms in schools

The idea of every teacher taking responsibility for the progress of all the children they teach is nothing new for most primary teachers, but may have been more of a change for subject teachers, particularly those working in large secondary schools, where they may be faced with a moving population of pupils large enough to make it hard to get to know the needs of each one. This is where communication systems within schools are important, so that there are strong links between all those involved with a pupil who has SEND. In terms of schools, this can be seen as putting the child at the centre, then the class or subject teacher, next the SENCO, and then the wider support and specialist expertise, with the engagement of parents and carers being key to the whole process (see Figure 1.1).

The change from having two stages of School Action and School Action Plus to a single stage known as SEN Support, provided an opportunity for schools to look again at pupils who have SEND and to move them into this category if the normal differentiation that is a feature of most classrooms is insufficient to address their needs and they require additional intervention or advice from other specialists. As mentioned previously, when this move was first established, the numbers of pupils in SEN Support were far lower than the numbers in the two previous categories put together. The important point is whether the provision is better because it is targeted at the right pupils, or whether there are learners who are missing out on the help they should have. At the moment, it is too soon to tell whether this is a blip, a downward trend, or whether figures will stabilise at around 15% rather than 18% of the school population.

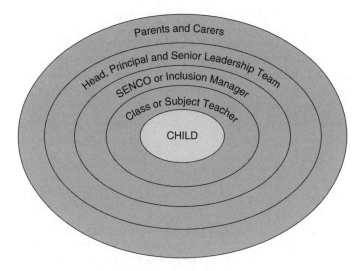

Figure 1.1   A 'team around the child' approach in a school setting

Source: Adapted from a PowerPoint slide by the DfE – 'A DfE presentation pack for school leaders: The 0–25 SEND Reforms'. It is available in the Resources section of the SEND Gateway (www.send gateway.org.uk/resources).

The need for nursery schools and all mainstream schools to have a SENCO who is both a qualified teacher and holds the National Award for SEN Co-ordination remains the same. However, the content of the training is changing to reflect the SENCO's more strategic role. The amount of hands-on support they are able to give will depend on the size of the school, any other roles they have, and whether they are a lone figure or in charge of a sizeable department. Although the role will be very different in different schools, the strategic overview they have should be much the same.

Activity

If you are working in a school, think about the following roles and how they function in your setting in terms of the support given by them to learners with special needs:

- The head or principal and the senior leadership team
- The SENCO (or inclusion manager)
- The class or subject teachers
- The teaching assistants who work with SEND pupils
- The SEN governor.

(Continued)

(Continued)

Once you have jotted down some notes, discuss your thoughts with a colleague. For instance, is there good communication between all concerned or do improvements need to be made, and, if so, how do you suggest this might be achieved?

The Local Offer and the SEN Information Report

In the same way that the Local Offer is a new requirement for LAs, the SEN Information Report is a new requirement for schools. The details of what each has to cover are set out in the SEND Code of Practice 2015 and in the relevant Regulations. The Local Offer is a great idea for providing information in one place for parents and carers, giving details of the SEN support services available in their area. It should also include information about support in other areas that the LA uses. For instance, few LAs will have the full spread of specialist provision for every type of need, so may draw on other LAs for low-incidence needs such as hearing or sight impairment. Although the Local Offer is a web-based resource, some LAs have gone to considerable trouble to produce their Local Offer in other formats as well.

The downside of the Local Offer is the huge variation in the way each one is presented. Although they have to include the same information, there are considerable differences in where it is to be found. This can make it difficult to navigate and to compare one Local Offer with another. While the Children and Families Bill was still going through Parliament, the Education Select Committee recommended that the Local Offer should have minimum standards and a national framework to ensure greater clarity and consistency. If this suggestion had been taken up, the Local Offer would have been more user-friendly and, perhaps, better known. Recent surveys have shown that there is a long way to go until the majority of families know about the Local Offer, let alone realise that it can be a very important source of information.

Initially, there was also some confusion about the link between the Local Offer and the SEN Information Report. Some LAs started talking about a School's Offer, instead of making it clear that the Local Offer is an LA responsibility, while the school's responsibility is to contribute to it. In practice, this has usually meant that schools link their SEN Information Report to the Local Offer as their contribution, rather than needing to provide anything extra.

Although there is also variation in how schools have presented their SEN Information Report, this is less of a problem, as it is fairly easy to see whether or not the 13 points set out in the Code and in Regulations have been covered, while a Local Offer is on an entirely different scale. Some schools have managed to enliven their Reports with photographs and audio or video clips of pupils and parents giving their views on the school's provision for SEND and what it has meant for them. While there is no requirement for them to do so, it does help to bring the information alive and may have the added bonus of catching the eye of Ofsted inspectors.

It would have been helpful if, from the start, the DfE had clarified the links between the LA's Local Offer, the school's SEN Information Report and the SEN/SEND policy that most schools have. While the latter is not statutory, having a policy provides a vehicle for giving the finer details of how the school organises its work in this area and, as well as being useful for parents, ensures that staff and governors are also clear about their roles and responsibilities.

'Not the same for all, but equal opportunities to succeed.'

The opportunities that were missed

The SEND Reforms were a major overhaul of the entire SEN system, so perhaps it was inevitable that, once they began to be implemented, some omissions would become evident. Those that spring to mind are:

- the failure to sort out SEN and SEND
- the lack of any consideration being given as to whether SEN/D should be part of a broader concept
- the lack of recognition for students in Higher Education
- the absence of any attempt to define inclusion
- the failure to promote the benefits of using a continuum of provision in more flexible ways.

SEN, SEND or a broader description

Taking together the first two bullet points mentioned, labelling people in any way is inclined to be controversial, but it is helpful to have the language to discuss children and young people's different needs and to recognise those who will require extra support. There are two issues around how to refer to pupils who need something over and above what is provided for the majority. The first of these is when to refer to SEN and when to add disability as well. The second question is whether it would be more helpful to set SEN/D in a wider context, as happens in Scotland and is being discussed in Wales.

In the Warnock Report of 1978 and the subsequent Education Act of 1981, 'special educational needs' or SEN became established. At that stage, the overlap with disability was not considered. However, it was made clear that pupils with English as an Additional Language (EAL) were not to be included with the SEN population. Quite rightly, there was a concern about differentiating between a child who was not fluent in English and the child with special needs. On the other hand, there is bound to be a degree of overlap, in that a proportion of EAL children, as with most other groups of children, will have special needs as well. As mentioned in the introductory chapter to this book, the SEN and Disability Act of 2001 sought to bring these two terms together, but a lack of clarity remained.

In 2013, the legislation needed to bring about the SEND Reforms became a major part of the Children and Families Bill. Originally, Part Three was headed 'Children and Young People with SEN'. After some amendments had been accepted, the title of the section was changed to 'Children and Young People with SEN or Disability'. As disability was a late addition, it is woven into some, but not all, of the SEND Reforms. For instance, for the first time, there is a SEND Code of Practice, but the new requirement for schools to produce a SEN Information Report has no 'D' in the title. As this was a time of a major review of the system, it seems an omission not to have clarified the terminology. It could also have been an opportunity to look at whether SEND would be a better term than something that would encompass all those in need of extra vigilance or support. Scotland's term of 'Additional Support Needs' (ASN) was mentioned in the previous chapter and came into being as a move away from SEN. This broader term encapsulates four factors:

- the learning environment
- family circumstances
- disability or health need
- social and emotional factors.

These headings encompass both short- and long-term needs. They include being in care, a young carer or from a service family; being bullied or bereaved; being an irregular attender; being a refugee or an asylum seeker; being from a travelling community or having English as an Additional Language (EAL); or being gifted.

Since the 2001 SEN and Disability Act, 'SEND' as a term began to be used, and the Children and Families Act 2014 has given a further push in this direction. However, far from any agreement about which pupils might have SEN but not be disabled, or not be disabled but have SEN, there is little agreement as to whether there are, in fact, two or three overlapping groups. So, some recognise that there are those that fall under the definition of disability but do not have SEN. Others recognise a third group as well, who meet the definition of SEN but are not disabled. This is illustrated in Figure 1.2.

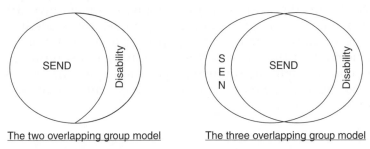

The two overlapping group model   The three overlapping group model

Figure 1.2   SEN and disability

Where there is a measure of agreement is in the overlap between SEN and disability being far greater than either being present without the other. On those grounds, therefore, it may be better to use the term 'SEND' in preference to 'SEN' as a general rule.

Going for a wider definition within which SEND is a significant component is less straightforward. The Equality Act recognises nine groups that have protected characteristics (see the previous chapter). This does not include SEN. Ofsted lists who inspectors see as belonging to 'vulnerable groups', which is similar to the list for Scotland's ALN. While there is no agreement on the way forward, schools are tackling it in different ways, one of which is to have an Inclusion Manager, either instead of or as well as a SENCO. As England continues to have SEN/SEND enshrined in law, it may be better to park the discussion for now, while keeping in mind the advice of Nancy Gedge. She is both a teacher and the parent of a child who has Down's syndrome, and wrote on the Special Needs Jungle website: 'Once we have the labels we need to peel them off the children and put them back in their boxes' (www.specialneedsjungle.com).

Higher education (HE)

Although there was a general welcome for the extension of special needs up to the age of 25, there was some dismay that higher education was not included in the Children and Families Act. The needs of students in further education (FE) are recognised, but not HE. This could be seen as another missed opportunity. It is not uncommon to come across students who have dropped out of their university courses, not because they had difficulty with the work, but because the support they needed was not forthcoming. While some universities do an excellent job in supporting their students with SEND, others are less accommodating. In some cases, there might be quite a cost attached to the support a student needs, such as a British Sign Language (BSL) interpreter, an expensive piece of equipment, or adaptations to the physical environment. In other examples, it may have been less about needing expensive support and more about knowing who to turn to for advice. Some universities have developed imaginative provision, for example, for students on the autism spectrum, but here was an opportunity to make it more of a level playing field rather than leaving it up to individual institutions. There is an unacceptably high rate of unemployment amongst those with SEND and this is one way in which more young people might have gone on to worthwhile careers.

Clarifying inclusion

Perhaps the most disappointing feature of the SEND Reforms was the failure to spell out a common understanding of inclusion. The sensitivities around the word became apparent when there was a strong reaction to the Green Paper that led up to the Children and Families Act 2014, stating it would be 'removing the bias towards inclusion'. This was widely assumed to mean that the Coalition Government (2010–2015) would reverse what it saw as the previous Labour government's policy of wanting to increase the placement of pupils with SEND in mainstream schools and reduce the number of special schools. In the event, the phrase did not appear in the Act, but by trying not to upset anyone, the government seemed to please no one. Although the people who had campaigned to have the phrase removed were pleased with the result, they still felt that there was too much emphasis on a positive future for special schools and a parent's right for their child to attend one. On the other hand, those who had hoped to see a more level playing field by the retention of the phrase, were disappointed that this would no longer be the case and that special schools might continue to be viewed as a second-best option.

The other interesting point about the use of the phrase 'bias towards inclusion', is that when it appeared previously in the Conservatives' Manifesto 2010, the words 'in mainstream schools' were added, making it quite plain that this was a reference to the process of inclusion and not to a place. As it was, the Act missed an opportunity to clarify what inclusion should mean and, instead, muddied the waters further by keeping the presumption of mainstream education for pupils with SEND, while also stressing that parents should be able to exercise choice.

Other emerging views

One year on from implementing the reforms, two interesting accounts appeared that also tried to summarise their early impact. Nick Peacey's (2015) discussion paper, 'A transformation or an opportunity lost?', was mentioned in the previous chapter. He argued that, while the reforms do enhance aspects of the previous SEND Framework, they fail on several points, including:

1. There are inadequate safeguards for introducing the reforms into an environment which is largely hostile to inclusion and equality.
2. They take insufficient account of research into the infant brain, which is beginning to challenge the resources that are available.

His first point raises the question of the context for the reforms. The attempts by successive governments to raise standards by piling pressure on pupils, staff and schools to meet ever more rigorous academic targets, and the effect this has particularly on children and young people with SEND, will be taken up in other chapters. The second point about a more complex population starting to emerge is one of the themes in the next chapter. Peacey also suggests that: 'The numbers of disabled learners learning alongside everyone else stalled around 2008' (2015: 8).

The other document was *Joining the Dots: Have Recent Reforms Worked for Those with SEND?*, which was commissioned by the Driver Youth Trust (DVT) charity (2015). One of the overriding concerns here was the fragmentation of the wider context, including:

- Changes to LAs' role and personnel
- An emerging but disorganised middle tier, including multi-academy trusts (MATs), Regional Schools Commissioners (RSCs), Teaching School Alliances, etc.
- A disparate school funding system
- Isolated and opaque schools.

The report argues, as does Peacey, that there was no point in looking at the SEND Reforms without considering the context and at how the unprecedented upheaval in the education sector as a whole has affected children and young people with special needs. It is not just structures that need to change, or even a culture of placing children and families at the centre, but the education system as a whole, so that it is not in a constant churn of change. However, even if the reforms do not achieve everything they set out to do, perhaps there are better times ahead than when a journalist, who was used to working in the trouble spots of the world, remarked that she found it easier being a correspondent in a war zone than getting the support her daughter needed for her autism.

Summary

After discussing the origins of the SEND Reforms and what they have achieved so far, a mixed picture emerged. On the positive side, parents and carers have reported that they value a more personalised approach, although the time this has taken has proved problematic for some LAs as they try to meet deadlines.

In terms of the theme of this book, it was disappointing to find that discussions about the meaning of inclusion had been avoided. While this could be seen as preferable to reigniting the debates at the end of the last century, there are drawbacks to this approach. Without complete clarity about inclusion and a commitment to having a flexible continuum of provision wherever a pupil is educated, progress could be held back by a lack of a common understanding of the route forward.

Further reading

Cheminais, R. (2015) *Rita Cheminais' Handbook for SENCOs*. London: Sage.

DfE (2015) *Special Educational Needs and Disability Code of Practice.* https://www.gov.uk/government/uploads/system/uploads/attachment_data/file/398815/SEND_Code_of_Practice_January_2015.pdf

Driver Youth Trust (2015) *Joining the Dots: Have Recent Reforms Worked for Those with SEND?* http://driveryouthtrust.com/wp-content/uploads/2015/10/DYT_JoinTheDotsReport October2015.pdf

Tutt, R. and Williams, P. (2015) *The SEND Code of Practice 0–25 Years: Policy, Provision and Practice*. London: Sage.

2

Why more specialist provision is needed rather than less

'The brain cannot be ignored when discussing development that is different.'

Chapter overview

Rather than reducing the continuum of provision by closing special schools, this chapter argues that specialist provision in all its various forms should be increased. The following reasons are given:

- The need to make a reality of early intervention
- The rise of a more complex population
- A demand for more specialist places
- A growing number of vulnerable children who may or may not have SEND.

Case studies are provided to demonstrate the benefits of settings, which, whether mainstream or specialist, provide an inclusive setting for a wide range of needs, as well as taking on a wider role.

The importance of the early years

The first three years of life are particularly important in terms of the development of the brain. Not only is it a time of rapid growth, but there is a direct relationship between the way in which the brain develops its physical structures and the infant's social and physical environment. This can be seen, for instance, in how a child's language ability develops. Infants from more deprived environments will arrive at school with far smaller vocabularies, perhaps unable to speak in sentences or knowing how to hold a conversation. A limited vocabulary means having fewer words with which to think and build up concepts. This also leads to a greater difficulty in becoming literate. Less obvious, perhaps, but also significant is the danger of having less emotional control, because the child does not have the vocabulary with which to express his or her feelings.

Key information: Neuroplasticity

Neuroplasticity is the term used to describe how the human brain changes its neurological structure in response to environmental influences and life experiences.

This ability, although present to some extent throughout life, diminishes significantly with age, the first three years of life being the time when the plasticity of the brain is at its height.

By the age of 5, the gap in achievement between those from a lower socio-economic status compared to those from a more advantaged background, is clearly evident. Schools can and do make a difference, but there may be limits to how far the gap can be closed.

This is why the early years are so important in determining the life chances of a child. For infants accessing early years provision, having highly trained and experienced practitioners will make all the difference. This has been recognised and the government has said that in 2016 it will review progression routes to determine what more can be done to enable good quality staff to maximise their potential and forge a successful career within early years provisions. There are other positive moves, too, such as the increase in health visitors.

Key information: Health visitors

In 2011, the Coalition Government promised it would increase the number of health visitors by April 2015. Before this, numbers had been going down. There are now over 4,000 additional health visitors, which was the government's target.

> This increase has made it easier to bring in an Integrated Review from September 2015, for 2–2½-year-olds. This brings together the former Healthy Child Programme and the written summary for parents required by the Early Years Foundation Stage (EYFS) Progress Check.
>
> In October 2015, NHS England transferred the commissioning of services for children between the ages of 0 and 5 to local authorities (LAs). This includes health visitor services.

Health visitors and children's centres

The fact that many health visitors are based in children's centres is an example of how much more effective support can be when it is joined up, not least in encouraging 'hard to reach' families to use their local children's centre. However, there are concerns that the vital work of children's centres may be at risk. Launching its annual Children's Centre Census for 2015, the national charity 4Children, (www.4children.org.uk) expressed its concern about continuing budget cuts and the pressure this was putting on the children's centres to target families with the highest need. Commenting on the findings, Imelda Redmond, Chief Executive at 4Children, said:

> Over a million families across the country use children's centres. No other part of our national infrastructure offers the same opportunity to identify and address problems early. Our census shows that cuts are directly impacting on children's centres' abilities to reach out and support families. (Imelda Redmond, 4Children, http://www.4children.org.uk/News/Detail/Cuts-to-over-2300-childrens-centres-put-help-for-struggling-families-at-risk)

Extra provision in the early years

Under the Childcare Act 2016, the 15 hours free childcare for 3- and 4-year-olds is doubled for working families, in addition to the 15 hours already offered to eligible 2-year-olds. The extra hours will become available from September 2017, with implementation in some areas a year earlier.

Extended schools and wraparound care

It is many years since governments started to talk about the Extended School, since when most schools have offered some or all of the following:

- Breakfast clubs
- Lunchtime clubs
- After school clubs
- Play schemes and holiday clubs.

Extended schools are designed to help make it easier for parents to be in work and also to offer a wider range of experiences and activities. These are of particular value for children whose lives would otherwise be very restricted. A more recent development is a consultation on schools offering wraparound childcare on their premises or nearby from 8am to 6pm, if parents request it and there is sufficient demand. Some schools have already been providing this themselves, while others out-source the provision, for instance to individuals, playgroups, or other private childcare providers. If schools can demonstrate that there is little or no demand for extended services, the consultation says that they can signpost parents to other local provision, such as childminders or nearby out of school clubs. Since September 2014, Ofsted has had a separate grading for early years provision, in the same way that a school's sixth form receives a separate grade and both may influence the school's final grading. In its document, *Inspecting Extended School Provision* (April 2014), Ofsted states that: 'Inspectors will want to consider how far these are enabling pupils to overcome specific barriers to learning and promoting improvements for all pupils and groups of pupils'.

One of the schools that has recently extended its age range to provide for very young children and has also had extended provision for many years, is Bignold Primary School and Nursery in Norwich. (There is further information about this school in the next chapter.)

Case study

Bignold Primary School and Nursery

The school has over 400 pupils on roll and caters for a very wide range of needs.

Fireflies Nursery is a grant-maintained nursery which is run by the school. It caters for 3- and 4-year-olds and holds a morning and afternoon session each weekday during term-time, providing for 26 children in each session.

Additional provision has been created for 2- and 3-year-olds, which is known as **Bignold Butterflies**. Originally managed by a committee it is now part of the school and runs on similar lines to the Nursery, with two sessions a day catering for a total of 40 children.

The school provides information for parents who want to know more about their eligibility for free childcare.

In addition, the school runs a **Busy Bees programme** offering quality play and care provision for 4- to 11-year-olds, both before and after school. There is also a holiday activity scheme throughout the summer holidays.

Clare Jones, the head teacher, works closely with the nearest children's centre in making sure 'hard to reach' families know about the opportunities available in the two settings.

Early years pupil premium

Another way in which early intervention has been supported is the introduction of the early years pupil premium, which is targeted at children from disadvantaged homes. It is a welcome extension of the pupil premium for school-aged children, which has been in existence since April 2011. When introducing it, the childcare minister, Sam Gyimah, said:

> The early years pupil premium gives money to providers so they can make sure eligible children have the best possible outcomes when they start school and beyond. The early years count and it will be life-changing for many of these children. (GOV.UK press release 2015)

Summer-born children and SEND

Before leaving the early years, it may be helpful to mention the position of children born in the summer months. It has been a concern for many years that summer-born children may be classified as having SEND simply because they are not ready for school, and then continue throughout their schooldays as one of the youngest in the class. In September 2015, Nick Gibb, the Schools Minister, said that the government wished to amend the School Admissions Code to make it clear that any decisions should be made in the best interests of the child and the views of the parents. In a letter to parents, LAs, schools and admission authorities (September 2015, GOV.UK website, The admission to school of summer born children), he wrote that, subject to consultation and Parliamentary approval, he wanted 'To ensure that summer born children can be admitted to the reception class at the age of five if it is in line with their parents' wishes, and to ensure that those children are able to remain with that cohort as they progress through school, including through to secondary school'. When everything in the school system is based on age, this may cause problems for some schools, but it is an example of the kind of flexibility that is a theme of this book as one of the ways in which the diversity of children's needs should be met.

Meeting the needs of a more complex population

Since the 1980s, there has been a discussion about reducing the number of specialist places, as mainstream staff become more skilled at meeting a wider range of needs. While there is no doubt that those working in main-stream settings have become used to educating pupils who might previously have attended special schools, there is also no doubt that the education service is faced with a more complex pupil population. It is for this reason that it makes sense to ensure that there is a range of provision within which every child can find somewhere that meets their needs and where they can feel they belong. Particular pressure points are the increases in children diagnosed with autism; a rise in mental health conditions; and the effects of a growing population of pupils born very prematurely. The first two of these will be addressed in a later chapter.

Prematurity

One way in which it is evident that the pupil population has become more complex, lies in the skill of the medical profession in enabling children to survive very serious accidents and illnesses, in a way that would not have been possible in the past. However, in some of these cases, children and young people may be left with SEND. Even more noticeable is the rise in the number of babies who survive being born increasingly prematurely. In 2014, the World Health Organisation (WHO) defined premature births as follows:

- Any birth that takes place before 37 weeks (i.e. three weeks before being full term)
- 32–37 weeks is moderate to late pre-term
- 28–32 weeks is very pre-term
- 28 weeks is extremely pre-term.

In addition, one in 100 babies is born alive between 22 and 28 weeks of pregnancy, yet a baby can be legally aborted up to 24 weeks. Research, such as the EPICure studies (www.epicure.ac.uk), which started in 1995, suggests that, whilst the rate of premature births has remained at much the same level in recent years, what has changed is the increase in survival rates, particularly of the very early-born group. Nearly half the babies born before 27 weeks now survive and of these, 45% will have a significant cognitive impairment, while the rest may have only minor difficulties. 'Bliss' (www.bliss.org.uk), a charity that describes itself as: 'for babies born too soon, too small, too sick', confirms that there has been this increase in survival rates. Barry Carpenter (2015), who, with colleagues, has studied the effect of these changes on educational settings, explains that:

> Any of these children are 'wired differently'; children born prematurely, particularly those of pre-28 week gestation, are a particular example of this phenomenon. Their profile of learning is not that which we have previously known with children with SEND (Carpenter et al. 2015).

An increase in children born very early has led to a number of schools for pupils with severe learning difficulties (SLD) and profound and multiple learning difficulties (PMLD) being extended or rebuilt. An encouraging sign in developing a better continuum of provision has been the number of new builds that have included the co-location of mainstream and special schools. The first of two examples in this chapter is a development in Wirral, which involves a mainstream primary school and a special primary school. The schools are not simply co-located on the same site, but physically attached.

Case study

Pensby Primary School and Stanley School

Pensby School opened its new building in May 2012, having previously been an amalgamation of three primary schools. There are 350 pupils aged 3–11. The school offers a free nursery facility, wraparound care for 3–5-year-olds and many extended activities, including breakfast and after school care.

Stanley School followed by joining Pensby in September 2013. This enabled it to expand its provision to cater for over 100 pupils aged 2–11 with a wide range of complex needs, including SLD, PMLD and autism.

The schools have been built in the shape of a horseshoe, so that each has its own section, with the central hub providing a range of shared facilities, including swimming pools, school halls and a dining room. This has enabled both schools to benefit from a better resourced environment, as well as providing opportunities for the pupils from both schools to be part of a wider community.

Stanley School had a long-established Inclusion Project with a different school before the move and so has been able to build on that experience. The benefits to the individual of inclusion are measured systematically and are mapped against the amount of involvement a pupil has in the activities that are offered and the degree of interaction with other children and adults that takes place. Activities that have been monitored in this way include: sports and swimming lessons, music and other lessons, playtimes, play sessions and lunchtimes.

Tony Newman, a former head teacher at Stanley School who set up the Inclusion Project, said: 'The school has always believed strongly that pupils in different provision need not be segregated or isolated from the community. The co-located building has made it easier to ensure that they feel fully included and valued'.

Rare syndromes

Moving on to other types of needs that are becoming more apparent, we now look at the rise in rare syndromes. It may seem slightly strange to talk about rare syndromes becoming more common, but, as it explains on the Unique website for chromosome disorders (www.rarechromo.org), individually rare chromosome disorders are very rare, indeed some are unique, but collectively they are common, with at least one in every 200 babies being born with a rare chromosome disorder. As the latest technology means it is easier to detect conditions arising from extra, missing, or re-arranged chromosome material, it is impossible to know how many have always existed, or whether there is a reason for the number to have multiplied. A chromosome disorder that is quite well known and understood is Down's syndrome, but many are more complex in their composition and are still being unravelled.

Contact a family (www.caf.org.uk), a national charity which has been supporting families with disabled children across the UK since the 1970s, suggests that 20 new rare conditions, including rare syndromes, are described every month. It adds that since the charity was founded, there has been a considerable increase in the number of families with disabled children. They put this down to the following factors:

- Improved diagnosis
- Better survival rates for pre-term babies
- A reduced stigma in reporting disability
- A broader definition of disability
- A rise in the number of children being diagnosed with mental health and behavioural difficulties
- Improved medical and palliative care.

While it is clear that there has been an increase in the number of babies born very prematurely and that many of these will have continuing issues, in the case of rare syndromes and some of the more recently recognised conditions, there is no way of knowing which really are newer and which ones have become recognised due to better diagnosis. In a way, it is ironic that the term 'special educational needs' came into being to concentrate on a child's individual needs rather than giving them a label defining the education they might receive, yet, today, there are far more 'labels' than when the Warnock Committee invented the phrase back in 1978. The following paragraphs give information on some of the conditions that readers may be less familiar with, although some were identified many years ago. (There is information on some of the better-known conditions in Chapter 5.) The ones covered here are listed in alphabetical order.

Attachment disorders

Babies and young children rely on parents or caregivers to meet their emotional and physical needs. This enables them to form a bond, to learn to love and to trust other people, to regulate their own feelings and to understand the feelings of others. In other words, they learn to become attached to other people. When their early needs as babies are not met, they may develop one of several types of attachment disorders. Looked after children (LAC), those who are adopted, or have suffered abuse and neglect, are particularly at risk. Young children who experience good quality care will know they are loved and lovable, and they will learn to trust their caregivers as people they can rely on. Children who experience poor care may see themselves as bad people who are worthless and unlovable. Furthermore, they will not establish trust in their caregivers and in other adults.

Feeling secure enables most young children to be well grounded and able to enjoy interacting with both adults and their peer group. If they are upset, they will go to a caregiver for comfort. On the other hand, those who do not trust adults to keep them safe may not turn to them for comfort. As there are many types of attachment disorders, the symptoms children display will be very different. Some will use attention-seeking behaviour to receive the notice they crave; some will exhibit loud and disruptive behaviour; and others will be quiet and compliant, while suffering in silence. Some will recoil from being touched or when shown physical affection. They may find it hard to show emotions themselves or appear to lack any sense of regret or remorse.

Complex learning difficulties and disabilities (CLDD)

This is one of the newer terms that arose from a two-year DfE project led by Barry Carpenter and resulting in a substantial online resource called the Complex Needs materials (www.complexneeds.org.uk). Unlike PMLD, where children will have very significant cognitive problems as well as a range of other sensory and/or physical conditions, CLDD is experienced across the whole of the ability range. However, what PMLD and CLDD have in common is that they include co-existing disorders. The definition of CLDD, which is quite lengthy, begins:

> Children and young people with Complex Learning Difficulties and Disabilities (CLDD) have conditions that co-exist. These conditions overlap and interlock creating a complex profile. The co-occurring and compounding nature of complex learning difficulties requires a personalised learning pathway that recognises children and young people's unique and changing learning patterns.

Where pupil engagement seems very limited, either because of significant cognitive difficulties, or due to disaffection, the Engagement Scale and Profile is a tool that was developed alongside the CLDD Research Project. It can be found in *Module 3.2 Engaging in learning: key approaches*, of the Complex Needs materials.

The other case study in this chapter involving a co-location is of a secondary mainstream school and a secondary special school in Wales. As in the previous example, the schools are physically attached, sharing facilities and opportunities for integration. This time the schools, which are in the Vale of Glamorgan, have a combined name – the Penarth Learning Community – and include a separate, onsite provision for respite care. The campus is seen as an asset for the whole community of Penarth. It provides a replacement for St Cyres secondary school and for the amalgamation of three special schools.

Case study

Penarth Learning Community

St Cyres is a comprehensive school for 1,100 pupils aged 11–18. The new building is on the site of the school of the same name, which needed to be replaced. The progress and welfare of each year group is overseen by a Director of Pupil Progress, who leads a team of support staff and a team of learning coaches. All pupils are interviewed individually by learning coaches every term. Sixth Formers help younger pupils with special needs and undertake a significant amount of voluntary work in the local community. Representatives from each year group form a Charity Committee, which, as well as fundraising, helps the pupils' social and emotional development.

Ysgol Y Deri is seen as a centre of excellence for autism education practice and caters for a range of children with very complex needs. The school has five trained learning coaches who work with students from 14 to 19, helping them choose their pathways and supporting them during transitions. Emotional literacy support assistants (ELSAs) are trained by educational psychologists (EPs) to support children with a range of emotional needs, including: emotional awareness, self-esteem, anger, social and friendship skills and loss and bereavement. They take groups or hold one-to-one sessions. A multi-disciplinary behaviour team from education and health works across the school to assist pupils in being ready to learn. The school has an outreach team consisting of education advisers and specialist learning support assistants (LSAs) who help in creating inclusive mainstream environments for pupils with autism.

Together, the two schools form the Penarth Learning Community, with shared facilities for sport and the arts, and specialist areas including a sensory pool and sensory rooms. During the process of the building being completed, School Construction Ambassadors were appointed from both the schools involved, reporting back to their fellow pupils on progress.

The final element of the Learning Community is the respite provision which is a 19-bed facility.

Chris Britten, the head teacher of the special school, describes his pupils as 'differently able'. He explains the aim of the school to parents as being to: 'Help and support you and your child by recognising their potential, creating opportunities for them and removing barriers to see them achieve to the best of their ability'. This is an important message, as one of the criticisms levelled at special schools by people who are less familiar with how they operate today, is that they don't prepare pupils for life beyond school. In fact, it is by giving them the skills they need to achieve maximum independence and by nurturing their sense of self-belief that they are helped to equip themselves for post-school life. (Further examples of co-located schools in different formats are given in Chapter 4.)

FASD and FAS

Continuing with the conditions that have become more talked about, foetal alcohol spectrum disorder (FASD), including foetal alcohol syndrome (FAS), is said to be the leading known cause of learning disability; yet, unlike almost every other special need, it is entirely preventable. If women did not drink when they were, or might be, pregnant, this is one condition that could be wiped out almost overnight. International studies suggest that one in a hundred children are born with FASD worldwide, but it may be higher in the UK because of the level of binge drinking among younger women. FAS is the most recognisable form, as it has a set of facial features – thin upper lip, flat nasal bridge, upturned nose, small wide-set eyes and no vertical groove (philtrum) between the upper lip and the nose. FASD may also have some physical effects which are less apparent, so the symptoms to watch out for include: difficulties with attention and memory; being hyperactive and having poor impulse control; difficulty with understanding maths and having weak problem-solving skills; immature behaviour and poor social skills.

In June 2015, an All-Party Parliamentary Group (APPG) for FASD (www.appg-fasd.org.uk) was launched and an *Initial Report of the Inquiry into the Current Picture of FASD in the UK Today* was published in December 2015. It has been known for some time that there is an unusually high number of children with FASD in the care system. The report goes so far as to suggest that: 'In essence, adoption in the UK could be said to have become predominantly a family finding service for children with FASD' (APPG for FASD 2015: 13). It is helpful that the chair of this APPG is Bill Esterson, the Labour MP for Sefton Central, who also chairs the APPG for Looked After Children and Care Leavers.

Key information: APPGs

There are hundreds of All-Party Parliamentary Groups (APPGs). These are informal cross-party groups of Members from the House of Commons and the House of Lords, who share particular interests. Many of them are supported by organisations from outside Parliament who act as the secretariat. Some of those that do useful work in the SEND field are:

22q11 Syndrome	Autism	Body image
Bullying	Complex needs and dual diagnosis	
Cystic fibrosis	Deafness	Diabetes
Disability	Dyslexia/SpLD	Epilepsy
Eye health & visual impairment	FASD	Learning Disability
Mental health	Speech & Language Difficulties	
Thalidomide	Young Disabled People	

The full list can be found under the Register of All-Party Parliamentary Groups at www.publications.parliament.uk – www.parliament.uk/mps-lords-and-offices/standards-and-financial-interests/parliamentary-commi ssioner-for-standards/registers-of-interests/register-of-all-party-party-parliamentary-groups/

The National Organisation for Foetal Alcohol Syndrome UK (NOFAS) can be found at www.nofas-uk.org

Activity

Work with a group of colleagues and look together at the list of APPGs. Select some that interest you.

1. Find out who is on the group and whether the group is active at the moment.
2. Check out any recent meetings or reports that are of interest.
3. Make notes on anything that might be useful.
4. Discuss these with any other colleagues who might be interested.

Fragile X

Although this is by no means a new condition, the extent of it has been recognised more recently and resulted in greater prominence. Fragile X is diagnosed through a blood test, so often goes undetected. It is a genetic condition which results in boys having a degree of learning difficulty while girls are often less seriously affected. Most children will need help with speech and language, as well as their social and emotional development. Other problems include delayed and distorted speech and language development, as well as difficulties with the social use of language. There may be repetitive behaviour, attention deficits and hyperactivity. In some individuals there may be other autistic-like features, such as poor eye contact, hand flapping, anxiety, abnormal shyness and an insistence on routine. Associated physical features are rarely obvious, but can include: a relatively large head, a long face with prominent ears, a large jaw and double-jointedness. Thirty per cent of people with fragile X syndrome are said to develop epilepsy. The Fragile X Society can be found at: www.fragilex.org.uk

Pathological demand avoidance (PDA)

Although this term was first used by Elizabeth Newson in the 1980s, it is only more recently that it has become better known. According to the National Autistic Society (NAS), PDA is now considered to be part of the autism spectrum, although people with this diagnosis have better communication and social skills and, unlike those with autism, know how to use these to manipulate other people. Features include: resisting any demands, excessive mood swings and obsessive behaviour. Most of all, they are very anxious young people whose anxiety leads to an overwhelming desire to feel in control of events. Unlike those with autism, they do not respond well to structure and routine, but need indirect approaches which involve negotiation; for instance, avoiding any question to which the answer can be 'no', but providing alternatives: Would you like to do this or that? The PDA Society has further ideas for helping these children to learn: www.pdasociety.org.uk

Sensory processing disorder (SPD)

SPD is the term mainly used in preference to sensory integration dysfunction. It has long been seen as a feature of other conditions, particularly autism. However, increasingly it is being recognised as a disorder in its own right. According to researchers at the Autism Research Centre in Cambridge, one in 20 children shows signs of SPD. Perhaps the even more surprising finding is that, while 80% of children on the autism spectrum have difficulties in this area, there is a larger group who have SPD but do not have autism (see Figure 2.1).

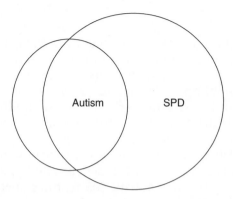

Figure 2.1   The overlap between sensory processing disorder (SPD) and autism

Source: Adapted from a PowerPoint on *Sensory Processing in Autism and the Built Environment* by Tavassoli and Brand (2011)

SPD results in a person having difficulty in processing information coming in from the senses and/or integrating the information being received. The information the brain receives through the senses helps the person to understand what is going on within their own body and in the world outside, so any distortion of this information can cause problems. There are varying levels of SPD, and in some cases only one sense may be affected, whereas in others it might be several senses.

As is common in those on the autism spectrum, a person may be hypo- or hyper-sensitive. So some will go out of their way to avoid certain sensations, while others will seek them out. For instance, a child with autism may want to sniff a person, while another may recoil in horror at the overpowering smell of the perfume or hairspray they are using. Usually, the senses of touch, hearing, vision, taste and smell, as well as movement and body position, occur automatically, without our having to think about how the nervous system is sending messages to the brain. This is an ability that develops more fully during childhood.

It is common to make a sensory profile of a child on the autism spectrum to check where any sensory difficulties lie. However, it is also worth using one of these profiles with young learners where this may be a source of anxiety or difficulty for them. Sensory profiles are usually divided into:

- Tactile (touch)
- Visual
- Auditory (hearing)
- Gustatory (taste)
- Olfactory (smell)
- Proprioceptive (awareness of body in space)
- Vestibular (balance).

There is one on the Autism Education Trust's website (www.autismedu cationtrust.org.uk, www.aettraininghubs.org.uk/wp-content/uploads/ 2012/05/37.2-Sensory-assessment-checklist.pdf). It has 50 questions that are quick to fill in, using: Yes, No, Don't know, plus a column for Action required.

Activity

Work with a group of colleagues and look back through all the information given on different types of needs.

1. Select one each that you are interested in learning more about and go to the relevant website.
2. Find out some more facts about how you might identify it and the strategies you might use to support learning.
3. Make a note of what you have discovered and share it with your colleagues.
4. Keep a note of what others have discovered that you think might be useful to you.

Catering for changing needs

The final case study in this chapter is of a special school for boys that has had to adapt to its changing population and, at the same time, expand its role to support staff and pupils in mainstream schools. It is well embedded in the local family of schools. For instance, it is in a federation of ten schools and one pupil referral unit (PRU) in Hampshire and is a strategic partner in the Solent Teaching School Alliance of 15 schools covering the 4–16 age range. The pupils' complex needs are less to do with their cognitive ability and more to do with mental health issues.

To address the complexity of need in its pupil population, the school has built up a multi-agency team, working closely with both health and social care. Despite their problems, most boys achieve qualifications in Functional English and Maths, and some are able to gain GCSEs in several subjects. This is made possible by the wide range of support they receive in managing their difficulties, which includes intensive family support, counselling, referrals to child and adolescent mental health services (CAMHS), to social services, and a range of other interventions. As one pupil commented to an Ofsted inspector: 'This school has opened doors for me. I can choose what I want to do and know how to get there'.

Case study

Prospect School

This is a community special school for 56 boys aged 11–16 who have social, emotional and mental health difficulties (SEMH). Many have additional needs including autism, PDA, ADHD, SLCN and learning difficulties (LD). Increasing numbers have severe mental health issues and are unable to attend full-time or are taught at home. Most KS4 students have college placements in a number of local FE colleges or attend part-time courses at other secondary schools in the federation.

The school has established a Multi-agency Wellbeing Team, which provides a range of therapeutic interventions for pupils and their families. As well as teachers and support staff, the team includes:

- A senior social worker and student social workers
- A family therapeutic practitioner and a trauma practitioner
- Counsellors, including a specialist grief counsellor
- Emotional literacy support assistants (ELSAs)
- An attendance officer
- An art therapist and a play therapist.

The team has made a real impact in engaging parents and carers and in improving attendance.

As many pupils have mental health issues, the head teacher, Marijka Miles, has worked with CAMHS so that the school can act as a triage service, prioritising the pupils with the greatest level of need. One of the assistant head teachers (AHT) is a trained social worker and the school has a second social worker on the staff as well. The AHT has an honorary contract with CAMHS and works with the CAMHS team for half a day every fortnight.

In conjunction with two other special schools, Prospect runs an outreach and consultancy service. This helps to maintain mainstream placements of pupils with behavioural and learning needs, as well as helping the schools to deal with challenging behaviour and other concerns. In addition, it has a training unit for social workers, in conjunction with the Universities of Chichester, Portsmouth and Winchester. The school is also is a Hub for supporting Havant's Troubled Families Programme. (This is a government programme to try to turn round the lives of families with a very significant range of problems.)

Marijka says: 'People often ask how many we return to mainstream education. My reply is that I don't see it as a badge of honour, although it might be a by-product of their improvement. We're seeing far more

> pupils with a lifelong disability, rather than pupils who can be turned round after a spell of intensive support in the right setting. In the last 5 years, there has been a change from those who will be able to hold down jobs to those whose lifelong disabilities will make this less likely'.

'Learn to accept difference but not indifference.'

Vulnerable groups

In the previous chapter, there was a discussion about whether or not children and young people with SEND should be seen as part of a larger category covering vulnerable groups in general. Whatever transpires by way of terminology in the longer term, schools and other services and settings are concerned about all those who may need greater support or attention. And it is often schools and other educational settings that notice if children are not being fed or clothed properly, suffer from other forms of neglect, or are distressed.

In Jacki Mitchell's school in Peterborough, Woodston Primary School, she operates a Vulnerable Pupils Register, which has its roots in the previous Excellence in Cities (EiC) programme. Jacki held a training session attended by all staff, including cleaners, lunchtime supervisors, kitchen staff and office staff. This provided a forum for sharing ideas, including a teaching assistant (TA) mentioning a girl's behaviour at playtime being completely out of character, while one of the kitchen staff had noticed that two children from the same family kept coming up for more helpings of food. From this pooling of information, six categories of concern were identified, which, again, built on the original EiC categories:

1. Attendance being less than 90%
2. Attendance being less than 85%
3. Child known to social services
4. Child having exclusions or periods of seclusion (internal exclusion)
5. Child's behaviour being a concern
6. Other

A referral form was designed and is now completed whenever a pupil is flagged by an adult in the school, a parent or the child themselves. This goes to the Learning Mentor, who is a trained counsellor, and if an intervention is felt to be necessary, over and above interventions to access the curriculum, a baseline is established at the start of the intervention, which might involve:

- Being put on the Register and monitored
- Alerting other agencies
- Adding the child to a Friendship Group or a Creative Work group, etc.
- Bereavement counselling or Talk Time with the Learning Mentor.

Pupils on the register are reviewed at least termly and de-registered when appropriate. At this time, exit assessments are carried out, so that there is a record of what has taken place.

Looked After Children (LAC)

A research project by the Universities of Bristol and Oxford, along with the Rees Centre for Research in Fostering, produced *The Educational Progress of Looked After Children in England: Linking Care and Educational Data*. This was launched at an event in November 2015. It was found that as many as 70% of children in care had SEN, with 20% being in special schools and a further 12% in PRUs.

Factors that exacerbated children's difficulties included:

- Having to move schools at the same time as having a new placement with a family
- Needing more support to achieve better attendance and to prevent exclusions
- Lack of staff's understanding of social, emotional and mental health problems
- Lack of close working between virtual schools, schools, social workers and foster carers
- A failure to include the young person in the decisions that affect them.

It is some time since every school was required to have a designated teacher for LAC and it is clear from this research that if the designated teacher and the SENCO roles are carried out by different people, there needs to be close working between them.

Virtual head teachers have recently been given responsibility for managing the allocation of the pupil premium, which is available to children in care as well as to the children of service families and those who are eligible for free school meals (FSM). Looked after children are usually placed on the roll of a virtual school, so that, although they will be scattered, their progress can be tracked as a group and as individuals by the virtual head teacher. All LAC children will have a Personal Education Plan (PEP) that records their personal history as well as their educational progress. The Who Cares? Trust is a voice for children in care (www.thewhocare strust.org.uk).

Summary

This chapter has emphasised the need for a continuum of provision from the early years onwards, in order to meet the needs of all young learners. The effects of babies born increasingly prematurely and the range of conditions recognised today, help to illustrate a growing need for specialist provision, rather than thinking in terms of reducing it. Several case studies were used to back up this approach.

The chapter ended with consideration being given to some other vulnerable groups, including children in the care system and the need to be on the lookout for any child requiring and deserving extra attention.

The next chapter moves on to consider how to make sure all parts of the continuum join together and support pupils, so that being bullied or finding themselves excluded becomes less likely.

Further reading

All-Party Parliamentary Group (APPG) for FASD (December 2015) *Initial Report of the Inquiry into the Current Picture of FASD in the UK Today* (www.appg-fasd.org.uk).

Carpenter, B. et al. (2015) *Engaging Learners with Complex Learning Difficulties and Disabilities: A Resource Book for Teachers and Teaching Assistants.* Abingdon: Routledge.

Ofsted (2014) *Inspecting extended school provision – Briefing for section 5 inspection.* April, ref.no. 100145.

Rees Centre (2015) *The Educational Progress of Looked After Children in England: Linking Care and Educational Data.* http://reescentre.education.ox.ac.uk/research/educational-progress-of-looked-after-children/

3

Creating a climate where all can thrive

'A range of rich environments in which a range of students can learn.'

Chapter overview

Following on from the previous chapter's discussion on why more specialist provision is needed rather than less, this chapter considers how different settings are adapting to meet the needs of their pupils. This includes:

- Parental views on provision
- How all schools are changing
- The dual role of special schools and the diversity of provision
- The importance of the right environment in terms of reducing bullying and avoiding exclusions.

The above points are illustrated by examples of what is happening in different mainstream and special schools, as well as developments in pupil referral units (PRUs).

What parents look for

In the 1980s and 1990s, parents were actively discouraged from seeking a special school place and it may have been true that, at one time, special schools prided themselves on being caring places rather than places of learning, but that has long since changed. The 1988 Education Act, which brought in a national curriculum and its assessment, as well as heralding the arrival of Ofsted, helped to ensure that special schools are held accountable for providing a broad, balanced and appropriate curriculum in the same way as any other type of educational provision.

In 2008, under the chairmanship of Brian Lamb, The Lamb Inquiry was established to investigate how parents could have greater confidence in the SEN system that was in place at the time. A year later, the *Lamb Inquiry: Special Educational Needs and Parental Confidence* was published. From this, it became clear that what parents said they were looking for was 'Someone who understands my child's needs'. A few years later, a similar point was made by Philippa Stobbs, when writing an article for the SEN Policy Research Forum, in which she pointed out that the level of skill and understanding was what attracted parents to a particular school, not the type of school it was: 'Parents did not want a mainstream school or a special school per se, they wanted and liked the place where they found the necessary expertise to meet their child's needs' (Stobbs 2012: 18).

A parent whose son is still at school, recently wrote as follows:

> As a parent of an adopted child with very complex needs we value the special school our son attends. My son by the age of six had been to 3 mainstream schools who just could not cope with him! If he hadn't had the chance to go to his current school, he would have been excluded from mainstream provisions. Although it was hard to get him in as his learning profile was too high, holistically our son needed staff who could give him an education that he deserves.

Another parent who had also experienced different placements for her daughter, summed it up like this:

> Despite the best efforts of highly inclusive and dedicated mainstream schools, special provision is invaluable and necessary in many ways. I think our daughter benefited enormously from what her special school offered in two principal ways. Firstly, the freedom to deliver a curriculum focusing on life skills such as budgeting, cooking, travel training, time telling and social skills prepared her for coping with the outside world. Secondly, her sense of being the same as everyone else improved her self-esteem greatly over the years she spent in special schools, particularly at secondary level. Other benefits of the school included personalised learning within the classroom setting and a high level of care concerning medical needs.

These comments from parents reflect the change commented on previously, that the swing towards an ideal of full inclusion in mainstream provision that was prevalent in the 1980s and 1990s, became tempered by realism after the turn of the century. So parents began to feel that they did not have to opt for a mainstream place, if their child had very significant special needs. Quite rightly, they focused on wanting a school where the staff would understand their child's needs and be most likely to be in a position to meet them. The key question of having better trained staff in all types of school is taken up in Chapter 5 of this book, both in terms of teaching staff and the growing importance of the role of teaching assistants.

Questions for reflection

'The 'ordinary' provision which will make the specialist less necessary'

1. Consider the thinking behind this comment, which was made by an LA school improvement adviser.
2. What are the ways in which this might be achieved?
3. Do you think it could reach a point where special schools would or should become redundant?

Adapting to a different population

This book argues that inclusion is a process that cuts across mainstream and special schools and that all types of schools have had to adapt to a more complex population of vulnerable pupils, including those who have special needs and disabilities (SEND). As a consequence, mainstream schools are now providing some of the approaches, facilities and resources previously found in special schools, while special schools have taken on expanding roles, both to meet the needs of their own more complex populations and to act as a resource for other schools and settings.

At the same time, as mentioned towards the end of the previous chapter, the way the education system has changed has made it a more hostile environment for those who happen not to be in the 'average and above' category in terms of their academic ability or who have other barriers to learning that make it harder for them to fulfil their potential. The constant testing and attempts to measure pupil against pupil have narrowed what children are taught and threatened to impact on their self-esteem. The fact that this has come at a time when, as shown in the last chapter, populations are becoming more complex and vulnerable, has been unfortunate. Nevertheless, some schools have gone out of their way to ensure all the children are taught in an environment where they can enjoy their learning.

Practical ways of creating an inclusive environment

The following examples show ways in which different schools have adjusted what they do to meet the needs of all pupils. The first case study is a primary school in Cumbria, where they have made it easier for all pupils to feel welcome, yet have still maintained high standards. In March 2015, its head teacher, June Venus, created the Building Futures Academy Trust together with Tebay, a nearby primary school, to develop innovative learning opportunities that would support the needs of small rural schools in isolated areas. The curriculum is skills-based and is built on the approach of Enterprise Education. (Further information about Enterprise Education can be found at www.enterprise-education.org.uk) The four key drivers are:

Enterprise (including Financial Education)

Creative Arts

Equality and Communities

Looking After Yourself and Others.

Case study

Yanwath Primary School, Penrith

Yanwath is a primary school for just over 100 pupils aged 4–11 years. It is set in a village in the north of the Lake District. The teaching is delivered as a whole school rather than in defined year groups or key stages. This allows children to race ahead or to have extra time to consolidate their learning, as does the focus on differentiating tasks to individual needs and allowing for different ways of working. Extra-curricular activities are made accessible to all. Pupils are asked about their learning and encouraged to say what helps them to learn and what they find difficult. Specific strategies are used when needed and include:

- Delivering the SEAL Programme (social and emotional aspects of learning)
- Having an in-school parent support adviser

(Continued)

(Continued)

- Running nurture groups
- Having 'chatting groups' for those who need more help with developing their communication skills.

Most pupils have their needs met in a classroom setting and staff are constantly improving their skills. They have been trained in the following intervention strategies: Reading Intervention; Maths Recovery; Makaton Level 2; Hearing Impairment Awareness level 1; Speech and Language; Team Teach; Smart Moves; and autism.

There is a Kids Consortium, whereby a number of Year 6 pupils work with the Senior Leadership Team (SLT) and take responsibility for aspects of school life. A House System enables older pupils to experience mentoring the younger ones. The school runs a breakfast club and an after school facility.

Commenting on the school's organisation one parent commented: 'I like the fluidity of the movement within their classes and the school as a whole in response to their learning needs'.

When asked what he liked about his school, one of the boys said: 'I like the teachers because they are not too strict and they are not too kind; they are in the middle'.

Although this is a relatively small primary school, the focus on staff having additional training to meet different needs is very clear and helps the school to meet a wide range of needs.

As an example of how special schools, as well as mainstream schools, have found it necessary to adapt their environments, the next case study is about The Valley School in Hertfordshire. In common with many schools for pupils with moderate learning difficulties (MLD), the school has been redesignated to cater for MLD, autism and speech, language and communication needs (SLCN). This has meant staff being trained to support this wider range of needs. The school has received Autism Accreditation from the National Autistic Society (NAS), and Elklan training for SLCN. (Both of these are explained further in Chapter 5.)

Case study

The Valley School, Stevenage

This special school has as its motto: Learn to believe; learn to achieve. It caters for well over 100 pupils aged 11–16 and has altered its environment significantly in recent years in order to cater for the needs of a more diverse population. Built round a series of open spaces, these have proved ideal environments for filling with a variety of flora and fauna, so that students can learn about horticulture and animal care and take qualifications in these areas. Inside the building, these spaces have been created:

The Globe: This is a newly developed multi-media resource base that is used for different lessons, including media studies, and by pupils during lunch breaks.

The Bridge and STEPS: These provide a KS3 and KS4 class for pupils needing a primary-based approach to the curriculum, with elements of a nurture group philosophy included.

The Link: This is a provision for pupils whose needs include specific learning difficulties (SpLD) and, in particular, dyslexia, which often goes undetected because it is overshadowed by the main presenting need.

The Den: This is a multi-sensory and 'chill out' place, both for pupils whose sensory issues need to be addressed and to provide an area from which the whole school can benefit in different ways.

The Hub: This is the most specialist area. Modelled on work done by Excellence in Cities (EiC), it provides an environment for a small number of pupils who are unable to cope with being full-time in a class. This includes pupils joining the school having been excluded and out of school for a long period of time; those who need an even more individualised curriculum plus a higher level of support; and those who use it part-time or during a crisis.

Speaking of her son's experience of using The Hub, one parent said: 'At puberty, everything seemed to change. I used to come into school in tears thinking things might not get better. Now he's much happier and achieves much more. He likes coming to school'. Her son, who has a diagnosis of dyslexia, dyspraxia and learning difficulties, added, 'I like it here. I think it's better for me. It's much calmer. I can do more art. I haven't always liked art, but now I'd like to go to art college'.

The head teacher, Corina Foster, explains that, as a society, we moved away from isolating children by putting them somewhere safe and hidden. Then we tried integrating them and making them do the same as everyone else. Now, we can change and adapt what we, as key adults, provide, making it possible for them to enjoy and achieve within this school and leave us with good prospects for the future. She says that when she shows round prospective pupils she tells them: 'This is a place where you can be yourself and where we will value you for who you are'.

Sensory circuits in special and mainstream schools

An example of how mainstream and special schools are exploring similar ways of changing what they do to support the needs of their pupils, is in the use of sensory-motor circuits. While the advantages of exercise are well known and many schools make a point of having periods of activity breaking up the school day, a greater awareness of pupils' sensory needs (as described in the previous chapter) means that activities such as sensory circuits are becoming popular. These consist of a series of activities designed to rouse the nervous system. They can be done at the start of the day, before or after a lesson, before or after a break time, or before going home. Each circuit falls into three parts:

1. Alerting activities, which provide input to arouse the nervous system and prepare it for learning.
2. Organising activities that encourage the ability to do more than one thing at a time (multi-sensory processing) and require planning and organisation of the body, as well as practice in improving balance.
3. Calming activities, so that pupils are ready to engage in a learning activity.

At The Valley School (which has just been described), the activities are mainly for individual pupils and some of the circuits will reflect this. For instance, the alerting activities might include jumping on a trampette or finding items in the ball pit. The organising activities might be about catching bean bags while on a wobble cushion or keeping a balloon in the air without letting it touch the floor. The final part might be doing a floor puzzle or lying under a weighted blanket. The time of the session is adjusted to the individual pupil, and each session is logged and commented on, so that progression can be evaluated.

At Woodston, a primary school in Peterborough (which was mentioned in the previous chapter for its work with vulnerable groups), sensory circuits are delivered in a group setting.

Case study

Woodston Primary School

This is a 4–11 community school for over 300 pupils. The school is keen to involve all its pupils by linking learning across subject areas through a Creative Curriculum. As the head teacher, Jacki Mitchell says, 'Children do not learn in compartments in their minds'. Learning is made as first-hand as possible through visits out of school and inviting visitors in to share their experiences and knowledge. Respect for the natural world is encouraged through an Eco Council and the school's own butterfly garden.

Care is taken to meet each child's needs and sensory circuits have been used for nearly a decade, when an occupational therapist (OT) trained two specialist teaching assistants (TAs) to deliver these sessions. There are two groups: 8.00am–8.30am and 8.30am–9.00am. One is for children who are hyperactive and one for those who need calming down. A baseline is taken and there is a half-termly assessment of the impact the intervention is having. These have shown that both behaviour and academic progress have improved.

The school has also been part of the 'Achievement for All' (AfA) initiative, which has encouraged increased parental engagement, particularly with parents and carers of children who have SEND or are underachieving. In addition, Woodston has been part of AfA's MITA project, looking at improving the work carried out by TAs.

Key information: Achievement for All

AfA: In recognition of concerns about the UK having a very wide attainment gap, with a long tail of underachievers, AfA was established to raise aspirations and improve the achievement of all pupils, particularly those facing barriers to their learning. There are separate programmes for early years, school, and post-16 providers, all of which are supported by Achievement Coaches from AfA.

MITA: This stands for **M**aximising the **I**mpact of **T**eaching **A**ssistants, a project that came into being in the wake of some research indicating that TAs could have a negative rather than a positive effect. Initially five schools took this on as a major project and found it was a very useful tool for improving teaching and learning.

(www.afaeducation.org)

The dual role of special schools

Few would argue against mainstream schools adapting what they do in order to provide for an increasingly wide range of pupils and, throughout this book, there are examples to illustrate some of the ways in which they have succeeded in becoming more inclusive. However, in the long-running saga about inclusion, it is special schools that have been in the firing line.

Some have argued for their closure, so that mainstream schools are made to become fully inclusive and able to educate every pupil regardless of the severity and complexity of their needs. While the debate has been rumbling on, special schools have been tackling their own twofold transformation: adapting to provide for the most complex end of the SEND continuum as it now presents itself and sharing their skills and expertise with colleagues in mainstream schools. This is not to suggest that specialist support services and other forms of specialist provision are not sources of support as well, but simply to stress the added value of special schools in taking on this dual role.

Special schools in Europe

It is interesting to note that this transformation of special schools from being accused of being segregated communities to becoming part of the continuum of provision, through having this dual role, is reflected in studies of special schools across Europe. For example, according to a study by Meijer (2010), 'Special Needs Education in Europe: Inclusive Policies and Practices', in countries such as Belgium, Greece, Spain, the Netherlands and Scandinavian countries as well as in the UK, special schools' role has been evolving from solely providing support to their own pupils to helping to build inclusive capacity in mainstream schools. Meier also noted that the northern European countries tend to have larger special school sectors. Numbers in special schools or full-time in special classes at that time, varied from 1% to 6%, with the average being around 2%. In the UK, although the number in special schools has been nearer 1.3%, this does not include other forms of specialist or resourced provision. What is interesting about these studies is the difficulty in producing a clear-cut figure for England, as the growing use of a flexible continuum of provision makes it harder to know where to draw the line. This could be taken as an encouraging sign that the discrete boundaries between special and mainstream schools, together with an interest in using all provision more flexibly, is taking shape.

The diversity of SEND provision

For many years now, successive governments have encouraged the growth of a more diverse school system. Since 2011, this has been further extended by the arrival of free schools. By the end of the year 2015, there were 350 free schools, with 17% being special schools or alternative provision (AP). Many more schools of all kinds are in the pipeline, so the present government is well on the way to meeting its target of having 500 free schools. This is part of the government's agenda to encourage parental choice and some of the free schools have been established by groups of parents, as well as other bodies. On the whole, the concept of free schools has been popular with parents, as evidenced by the number that have been oversubscribed as soon as they open. It is too early to say what their effect will be in the longer term. Although there was a reduction in the number of special schools between 2002 and 2009, there was no reduction in the percentage attending them. Since then, the picture is changing through the advent of special free schools and the growth in the general pupil population.

Key information: Special academies and free schools

Special academies are schools that have converted from being maintained or non-maintained special schools.

Special free schools are schools that have been established for pupils with SEND, using the same process as for other types of free schools. (All free schools are a type of academy.)

Unlike other special schools, it is possible to admit pupils without a statement/EHC plan, if a specified number of non-statemented places has been sought as part of the funding arrangement for a special academy.

Alternative provision (AP) academies are former pupil referral units (PRUs).

Charities, groups of teachers, existing schools and parents can set up these new schools if they can prove that they are needed and wanted by a local community.

Up-to-date information is provided on the New Schools Network (NSN): www.newschoolsnetwork.org

---

In *Special educational needs survey 2016 – guide for the completion of the SEN2 return, version 1.3* (DfE 2015i), there is a list of all the educational establishments where children and young people with SEND may be found. This includes:

- A range of maintained and non-maintained early years settings
- Resourced provision in LA maintained mainstream schools
- SEN units in LA maintained mainstream schools
- LA maintained, non-maintained and independent special schools
- Hospital schools
- LA maintained PRUs
- Specialist post-16 institutions.

The terms 'Resourced provision' and 'SEN units' are differentiated as follows:

Resourced provision has places reserved at mainstreams schools for pupils with a specific type of SEN. They are taught mainly in mainstream classes, but require a base and some specialist facilities around the school.

SEN units describe mainstream schools where children are taught mainly within separate classes.

Additional funding is available from the LA for both these types of SEND provision. The list gives an idea of how children and young people with SEND are embedded right across the education system.

The importance of the right environment

The final parts of this chapter consider how being in the right environment, whatever form that takes, can help to reduce the bullying of pupils with SEND and avoid unnecessary exclusions.

Bullying

Although it is not always easy to feel empathy for those who bully and cause distress to others, in fact bullies have often been bullied themselves or have other reasons for feeling angry or inadequate. Some of the main reasons for bullying include the following:

- A coping mechanism when life seems tough or friends are in short supply
- A feeling of insecurity
- Jealousy of the person the bully is targeting
- Prejudice against people who are different
- Concern about not being accepted if they do not join in with any bullying that is already going on.

What all forms of bullying have in common is that they cause distress to the person who is being bullied. As bullies often pick on someone they see as different, children with SEND can be a target. One of the reasons that parents may opt for a smaller or more specialist environment, is the fear that their child will be bullied. A particular problem for pupils with SEND is that their self-esteem is already inclined to be low because of the challenges they face and the last thing they need is to be bullied or feel rejected. There is also the argument that if children become used to being with those who have special needs, they will treat this as normal. This is the approach put forward by Clare Jones, whose school was mentioned in the previous chapter in connection with her early years provision.

'Including and inspiring everyone'

Case study

Bignold Primary School and Nursery, Norwich

The school prides itself on being inclusive. It is a single-storey building and prefers to have all pupils in class rather than some in a special unit. There are facilities and access for wheelchair users and visual timetables in every classroom. The school has pupils with a wide range of needs, including hearing impaired (HI), sight impaired (VI) and Down's syndrome.

Clare says that there is very little, if any, bullying because pupils are used to being with others who have special needs. This is backed up by a number of other steps the school takes:

- Teaching the children that it is never OK to say unkind words to anybody
- Having a very clear and comprehensive anti-bullying policy, which makes useful reference to the UN Convention on the Rights of the Child (UNCRC)
- Celebrating Universal Children's Day
- Taking part in anti-bullying week
- Training staff as 'Thrive Practitioners'*

*Thrive helps to understand the needs being signalled by children's behaviour and provides targeted strategies and activities to help them re-engage (www.thriveapproach.co.uk).

Two other factors are the very strong relationships with parents, which are encouraged through a family partnership worker and weekly 'Stay and Play' sessions in the Reception classes, with over 50% parental attendance each week. Secondly, the ethos throughout the school that bullying will not be tolerated and every child must be treated with respect by everyone, is constantly reinforced.

Clare would love to be able to say that she can cater for every pupil, but she says: 'I'm realistic if I can't meet their needs. With a very few, the distance grows and they become more isolated because of it. Academic needs can be met, but not necessarily the social and emotional needs, in which case, they will feel adrift'. However, to make sure they have the support they need, Clare makes maximum use of support staff and she has:

- **Learning Support Assistants (LSAs)**, who take on one-to-one support with pupils
- **Teaching Assistants (TAs)**, who support class teachers and help with small group work
- **Specific Intervention TAs**, who are trained to deliver different types of interventions, including Thrive.

Anti-bullying advice

The DfE regularly updates its guidance to school, the most recent version being: *Preventing and Tackling Bullying – Advice for Headteachers, Staff and Governing Bodies* (DfE 2014c, October 2014). Recent figures suggest that 30,000 fewer children in England are being bullied compared to figures obtained in 2005. The anti-bullying alliance has free online training for professionals, and a section with SEND Anti-Bullying programme resources (www.anti-bullyingalliance.org.uk).

Activity

1. Check the government's most up-to-date guidance on bullying and compare it with the policy on this issue in a school you know well. Discuss with a friend or colleague any changes you think should be made.
2. Go to the Anti-bullying Alliance's website and explore either the free online training or the SEND Anti-Bullying programme resources. Make note of anything it would be worth returning to later.
3. Find out more about Anti-bullying week and consider whether it might be useful for a school or setting you know. If so, make a list of the points that might persuade the school to participate next time.

'How to include and not exclude'

Exclusions

In the most recent Exclusions data sent to the DfE, *A Guide to Exclusions Statistics* (DfE, 2015c, July 2015), there is a list of the main reasons provided by schools for excluding pupils. The first one in the list links with the previous section:

- Bullying
- Damage to school or personal property or theft
- Verbal abuse or threatening behaviour towards another pupil
- Drug and alcohol-related issues
- Persistent disruptive behaviour
- Physical assault against an adult or a pupil
- Racist abuse and sexual misconduct.

Despite the DfE's guidance on not excluding pupils with SEN unless absolutely unavoidable, the July 2015 figures state that pupils with SEN, with and without statements or EHC plans, account for seven out of every ten permanent exclusions. Clearly, this is an area where more needs to be done, including making sure that young learners have the support they needs and are in a setting that helps them to respond positively to the opportunities offered.

Secondary schools, where bullying is inclined to be more of a problem, partly because of their size and partly because the teenage years are not the easiest time, have come up with various ways of making exclusions less likely. Impington is one of the village colleges in the South of Cambridgeshire that helped to pioneer comprehensive education in the 1930s. It has worked hard to ensure that no pupil is excluded and that there is suitable provision for everyone who attends, including arrangements for post-16 pupils who are not cut out to take the more traditional exams.

Case study

Impington Village College, Cambridge

The college has nearly 1,500 students aged 11–19. The college's strapline is: '*Inspirational – inclusive – international*'. Robert Campbell, the principal, aims to keep alive its pioneering spirit. His was one of the first schools to offer the International Baccalaureate (IB). He has implemented vertical tutor groups (mixed ages) and appointed a Head of Personalised Learning and Attendance as well as a SENCO.

The school has two specifically equipped resource bases to support the learning of pupils with SEND. One of these is for up to 18 pupils with physical disabilities that the school is funded to provide for. Here, there are hoists, a physiotherapy room and personal care facilities. The other is for pupils from Y7 to Y11 who can be given a wide range of support and interventions, including literacy and numeracy interventions, and several therapies including speech and language therapy, physiotherapy, occupational therapy, music therapy, hydrotherapy and lego therapy. There is a supervised social space at break times for those who need it.

At post-16, students with EHC plans are able to stay on, as there is a full-time two-year course housed in a purpose-built facility within the college. This is known as IDEAL, standing for Independence, Decision-making, Enterprise, Access to Employment and Leisure and Learning. There are links with the National Trust's Anglesey Abbey and Cambridge Regional College, so that students can follow a range of accredited courses, including ASDAN and BTECs.

The school's anti-bullying policy, 'Don't suffer in silence', explains that bullying is deliberately hurtful behaviour; that it is repeated over time;

(Continued)

(Continued)

and that an imbalance of power makes it hard for the bullied to defend themselves. The school's Good behaviour (Rewards and consequences) policy emphasises ways in which pupils' good behaviour for learning is recognised by all levels of staff.

Although there are some temporary exclusions, often as a result of swearing, in recent years there have been no permanent exclusions. Instead, the school has established internal mechanisms to try to avoid having to exclude. This includes isolating pupils for varying lengths of time, from a single lesson to several days, depending on the seriousness of the offence, and using internal exclusions as a second stage when needed.

As the school has its own internal procedures, it rarely uses any form of alternative provision (AP), although managed moves to one of the other village colleges may take place. For other schools, various forms of AP are an option when it seems impossible to keep a learner in their current school environment.

Alternative provision (AP)

Children and young people educated in these settings are among the most vulnerable pupils. They include those who have been excluded or who cannot attend mainstream school for other reasons, such as having a short- or long-term illness, being school phobic or a pregnant teenager or young mother, or simply because they are waiting for a school place when everywhere is full.

Pupil referral units (PRUs)

PRUs have been the most usual type of AP, although this is changing as they lose the name on becoming an academy (which they are encouraged to do) and are called an AP Academy. PRUs are LA establishments providing education for children unable to attend a mainstream school. The majority are likely to be pupils who have been excluded or who are at risk of exclusion. PRUs have a head teacher and are counted as schools. Since April 2013, PRUs have been given greater control over their budgets and staffing, so that they now have similar freedoms to mainstream schools. There have been many reviews of PRUs and different models have been tried to ensure all those attending them have every chance of receiving an education that puts them back on the road to success. At one stage, they were going to be called 'short stay schools' to emphasise that they should not be seen as a long-term solution. The White Paper, *Educational Excellence Everywhere*, (March 2016), states that, while LAs will retain responsibility for ensuring there are sufficient places, head teachers will become responsible for AP budgets, commissioning places and being accountable for the educational outcomes of pupils they have excluded.

The organisation for PRUs has changed its name to PRUsAP to encompass other forms of AP as well: www.prusap.org.uk

PRUs and special schools

One of the difficulties PRUs have faced has been the lack of clarity between alternative and specialist provision. As there is a high number of pupils excluded who have SEND (including some who have been in special schools), there is bound to be an overlap between PRUs and special schools, and particularly those who have pupils with what used to be termed 'behaviour, emotional and social development' (BESD) but since the SEND Reforms has become 'social, emotional and mental health difficulties' (SEMH).

The last case study in this chapter is of a group of former PRUs in Cornwall, which have formed a multi-academy trust (MAT). Robert Gasson is the CEO and Executive Principal of Acorn Academy which is made up of six regional AP Academies and one medical AP Academy. The latter is a Community Hospital Service. Robert says his focus is on mental health and wellbeing, but this is never used as an excuse and pupils are pushed to have aspirations and to succeed academically. He never excludes as there is nowhere else for the students to go, but can move them around within the MAT if this helps to give them a fresh start. If someone is too violent to be retained, there is online schooling that can be accessed and staff will monitor their progress and continue to support them. Local schools make up the placement panels and decide which pupils need to attend. The exception is the medical AP, for which there is a medical placement panel. KS2 and KS3 pupils are only expected to attend the APs for three or four terms before being reintegrated. KS4 students will be prepared for university, college, apprenticeships or employment.

Case study

Acorn Academy, Cornwall

All the AP Academies provide education for pupils who are seen as disengaged from education and who:

- have been excluded
- are at risk of being excluded
- need intervention.

(Continued)

(Continued)

The former PRUs that make up the MAT are:

North Cornwall near Camelford, which works closely with all the secondary schools in the north of the county and provides for KS3 and KS4 pupils

Nine Maidens in Redruth, which has both primary and secondary provision

Restormel which is based in St Austell and covers mid-Cornwall with provision from KS1 to KS4

Caradon based in Liskeard has KS2 to KS4 provision and serves south-east Cornwall

Glynn House is in the city of Truro and covers secondary provision (KS3 and KS4)

Penwith near Penzance is a KS2 to KS4 provision

CHES is the Community and Hospital Education Service based in Camborne. It is for pupils whose health needs mean they are not in school for medical reasons. These pupils are dual registered with their mainstream school and with CHES, which covers the whole county.

Pupils in Acorn Academy range from those who settle down and take several GCSEs to those whose behaviour is so challenging that they need time and a variety of therapeutic approaches before they can re-engage with learning.

Rob sees one of the current challenges as resulting from the unintended consequences of the government's push for subjects that form the English Baccalaureate, which has resulted in sports and the arts being seen as less important. As one mainstream head said to him: 'I don't want to narrow the curriculum but I can't see another way of meeting DfE targets'. Rob is also concerned with what he reckons in the last three years to be a 150% increase in the number of very young children being excluded. So he is on the receiving end of a much younger and more complex population. He explains: 'We will never limit children's choices and we will always try to put them back on a flightpath, despite what has happened to them in the past. After all, there is no alternative once they are in alternative provision'.

For whatever reasons, it is the case that there is an increase in the rise of very young children being excluded, together with a rise in mental health conditions. This makes it even more important to make sure a continuum of provision is in place, with the component parts working together to adapt to pupils' changing needs, to make sure no child falls through the gaps, and to place them in an environment where they have the best chance of success.

Summary

This chapter has illustrated how all types of schools and other settings have had to adapt what they do to meet the needs of a changing population. Case studies from across mainstream, specialist and alternative provision show how, between them, they are trying to keep up with changing needs and to provide for pupils in ever more diverse ways.

Ways of reducing bullying were discussed as was addressing the large percentage of pupils with SEND who are excluded.

There are encouraging signs that closer working across the continuum of provision, is producing a range of approaches and provision, including very young pupils and those who are being diagnosed with serious mental health issues.

Further reading

DCSF (2009) *Lamb Inquiry: Special Educational Needs and Parental Confidence.* http://webarchive.nationalarchives.gov.uk/20130401151715/https://www.education.gov.uk/publications/standard/publicationdetail/page1/dcsf-01143-2009

Larkey, S. (2006) *Practical Sensory Programmes for Students with ASD and Other Special Needs.* London: Jessica Kingsley.

Stobbs, P. (2012) 'Overview of Previous National SEND Achievements and their Fit with Current SEND Policy Directions', *The Coalition Government's Policy on SEND: Aspirations and Challenges?* Policy Paper, SEN Policy Research Forum. www.sen-policyforum.org.uk

Tutt, R. (2011) *Partnership Working to Support Special Educational Needs and Disabilities.* London: Sage.

Achieving a more responsive system

'Children's behaviour is a form of communication.'

Chapter overview

The previous chapter concentrated on how to provide an environment where the children within it could flourish, rather than being bullied or excluded. This chapter considers how different environments are working together to form a continuum of provision and using it more flexibly. After looking at opportunities post-16, the chapter covers:

- How special schools became embedded in the system
- How co-locations and partnerships are continuing to develop across former boundaries
- How individual packages of support are being offered.

Case studies include: a teaching school alliance across the sectors; a special school multi-academy trust (MAT); a Northern Ireland (NI) partnership of schools; and flexible packages of support, with one case study where every young learner has a bespoke package.

The continuum of provision

It was evident in the previous chapter that learners with SEN can be found in an increasingly wide range of provision. The advantages of having such a broad range is, firstly, that there are more options to meet different children's requirements. Whereas the vast majority of those with SEND will have, and always have had, their needs met in mainstream contexts, it has generally been recognised that the more complex children's needs are, the more vital it is to adapt the environment for them, rather than expecting that they will be able to fit in with what is provided for the majority. Secondly, the more options there are, the greater the possibilities for a flexible use of that continuum of provision. This is helpful, not just in finding an environment that suits each individual, but in being able to adapt that provision as their needs change. In addition, the continuum as a whole can be adjusted to reflect the needs of a changing population. For example, in a comparatively short space of time, autism has gone from being seen as a low incidence need to one of the five most common. (Autism is explored further in the next chapter.) Once any remaining barriers between mainstream and special schools have disappeared, there will be less resistance to the idea that pupils – and staff – can benefit from experiencing different environments, including the greater use of assessment placements, short-term, part-time or dual roll provision.

Increasing the provision for post-16

Since the original discussions about inclusion moved on from a distinct division between mainstream and specialist provision, to developing a range of different environments, there has also been the need to consider the extension of the SEND age range to cover the years 0–25. While the provision for pre-school children has been developing for some time (as described in Chapter 2), there has been a particular need to do more about post-16 and, particularly, post-19 pathways. In *Special educational needs survey 2016 – guide for the completion of the SEN2 return, version 1.3* (DfE 2015i), which was referred to in the previous chapter, provision for older learners in the form of apprenticeships, traineeships and supported internships is mentioned.

Key information: Apprenticeships, traineeships 0━ and supported internships

Since August 2013, all young people aged 16–19, or 16–25 for those with an EHC plan or Learning Difficulty Assessment (LDA), have been expected to continue studying, either full- or part-time.

Apprenticeships enable young people to combine paid work with being trained on the job, while gaining qualifications leading to a

(Continued)

(Continued)

career. As they are offered at Level 2 or Level 3, those who are below this level may need to start with a traineeship.

Traineeships are an education and training programme involving work experience. They can lead to an apprenticeship or other training in FE or elsewhere, or provide a route to gaining employment. They run from six weeks to six months.

Supported internships are designed for young people from 16 to 25 who have an EHC plan or LDA. Most of the time is spent in the workplace doing a real job, supported by a job coach and with a personal study programme as well.

A summary of current advice and information on supported internships is given in the DfE's (2014b) *Supported Internships: Advice for FE Colleges, Sixth Forms in Academies, Maintained and Non-maintained Schools, Independent Specialist Providers, Other Providers of Study Programmes and Local Authorities*. This was revised in December 2014, with the next review due in May 2016. Most students with SEND will be able to attend courses at their local college. Those with high levels of need may require courses below Level 1. These are described as: Pre-Entry Level to Level 3. For those who require a more specialist environment, there are colleges for a wide variety of needs. The Association of National Specialist Colleges (Natspec) (www.natspec.org.uk) has further information.

Activity

Find out what you can about:

1. Local options for pupils with SEND to stay on in the sixth form
2. The kinds of support offered by any local FE colleges.

Go to the Natspec website and find out more about the range of specialist colleges that exist and the types of need they support.

Joining up the sectors

As described in the opening chapter, in the 1980s and 1990s special schools and mainstream schools were seen as two very different sectors and terms such as 'segregated provision' for the former were often used. Once the concept shifts from inclusion referring to a place to being a process, all sorts of possibilities emerge. Evidence of this blurring between former boundaries is apparent in the way special schools have been increasingly included in developments brought in by successive governments, which have encouraged schools to work in partnership in order to raise standards. This gradual acceptance of special schools as part of a continuum of provision is exemplified through four initiatives, where special schools have been fully involved: the Specialist Schools Programme, Teaching Schools, National Leaders of Education (NLEs) and Academies.

The Specialist Schools Programme

This began in the 1990s and by the time a separate funding stream was abolished in April 2011, 95% of secondary schools had one or more specialisms. This, in itself, was a way of increasing the diversity of opportunity to meet the needs and talents of individual pupils. To begin with, it meant that secondary schools, and, a little later, special schools with secondary-aged pupils, could be recognised as having a specialism in one or two subject areas.

The SEN strand

In 2005, a new SEN strand was introduced in each of the four areas of need in the 2001 SEN Code of Practice, namely: cognition and learning; communication and interaction; behaviour, emotional and social development (BESD); and sensory or physical impairment. While special schools were keen to be recognised as having a SEN specialism, perhaps not surprisingly, few secondary schools put themselves forward. Although the separate funding stream was discontinued some years ago, many schools have continued to be recognised for their specialisms in areas of the curriculum or in SEN.

Teaching schools

A second development was the DfE's decision to have more initial teacher training (ITT) based in schools, as part of a move to what it refers to as a self-improving, school-led system. The DfE aims to have 600 teaching schools by March 2016, looks likely to be met. Teaching school status is open to all outstanding schools in England including:

- Nursery schools
- Primary, middle, secondary, all-through and special schools
- Pupil referral units (PRUs)
- Faith schools
- Independent schools
- Academies, chains and free schools
- Sixth-form colleges.

In addition, they may have strategic partners who lead some aspects of training and development. These may be other schools from any phase or sector; universities; academy chains; LAs; dioceses; and private sector organisations.

Teaching schools lead an alliance of other schools and have six core areas of responsibility:

1. ITT (initial teacher training)
2. CPD (continuing professional development)
3. Supporting other schools
4. Identifying and developing leadership potential
5. Specialist leaders of education (SLEs)
6. Research and development.

In March 2014, the National College for Teaching and Leadership's (NCTL) *Impact of Teaching Schools* publication gave examples of the ways different teaching school alliances have responded to the six areas of work. Singled out for mention in 'Identifying and developing leadership potential' is the Forest Way Teaching School Alliance, which is led by Forest Way, a special school in Leicestershire. As with many other teaching school alliances, it provides a good example of how the different sectors are working together.

Case study

Forest Way Teaching School Alliance

This teaching school alliance, which started in July 2011, involves 53 schools:

- 1 special nursery
- 6 special schools
- 39 primary schools
- 7 secondary schools.

Between them, they have over 13,700 pupils. The Alliance provides School Direct Initial Teacher Training in partnership with the University of Derby, University of Leicester and Loughborough University, in both primary and secondary teacher training, all the trainee places are with Alliance Schools. Going into the fourth year of IT Training for 2016/17 there are 16 primary trainees and 12 secondary trainees.

Forest Way also has a key role in talent development through its co-ordination of the Leicestershire SENCO network. Tailored professional development is offered in a wide range of areas such as support for looked after children (LAC), autistic spectrum disorders (ASD), dyslexia, Makaton and low-incidence SEND. Forest Way is also one of 20 Teaching Schools to be recognised as an Early Years Hub, which means it provides support and training for staff working with the youngest children in the alliance aged 0–4. This includes working with childminders.

NLEs, LLEs, SLEs and NLGs

The third example of special schools being embedded in the system is through head teachers of outstanding schools becoming National Leaders of Education (NLEs), in which case their school becomes a National Support School (NSS), or Local Leaders of Education (LLEs). They work either nationally (NLEs) or locally (LLEs), to increase leadership capacity in schools other than their own. Specialist Leaders of Education (SLEs) are middle or senior leaders in their own school who carry out a similar role with their peers in other schools. More recently, National Leaders of Governance (NLGs) were introduced. These are posts for experienced chairs of governors to support less experienced chairs. At present, there are about 400 NLGs. All these positions are available to people in mainstream and special schools, and form another way of showing that expertise is valued wherever it happens to be.

Academisation

Finally, academies entered the field in 2000, when their purpose was to improve the education of young people in disadvantaged areas who were in failing schools. Since then academies have taken many different forms. Although becoming an academy was originally only a possibility for secondary schools, the Academies Act of 2010 widened the field to include primary and special schools. Since then, other types of academies have appeared, with University Technical Colleges (UTCs) and Studio Schools offering a different style of curriculum to 14–19-year-olds and Free Schools becoming part of an increasingly diverse range of provision, as itemised in the previous chapter. Free schools can be set up by teachers, parents, existing schools, educational charities, universities and community groups. The advent of these schools has added to the diversity of provision for pupils with SEND, as this has been seen as one of the pressure points in the system. A newer development has been the appointment of Regional Schools Commissioners (RSCs). Originally, they were appointed to approve the applications for new academies and to oversee the performance of all the academies, including free schools, in their area. However, the Education and Adoption Act (2016) gives RSCs a wider role, which could overlap with that of Ofsted and local authorities (LAs).

Questions for reflection

Think about the four ways that have been described whereby the same opportunities have been offered to special schools as mainstream schools have had.

(Continued)

(Continued)

1. In each case, what do you see as the advantages *for* special schools?
2. What might special schools add to the drive for a 'self-improving, school-led system'?
3. Do you see these developments as entirely positive, or can you think of any drawbacks to including special schools in these ways?

Academy chains and multi-academy trusts (MATs)

As the number of academies has proliferated, some have become part of academy chains. By March 2015, over half the 4,000 or so academies were in these formal collaborative arrangements. Each academy has to form an academy trust, of which there are two types:

1. A single academy trust (SAT) which runs one academy
2. A multi-academy trust (MAT) which runs more than one academy.

In a Statistical Working Paper the DfE published in March 2015 (DfE 2015j, *Measuring the Performance of Schools within Academy Chains and LAs*), it suggested defining an academy chain as a group of five or more academies consisting either of separate SATs, MATs or a mixture of the two.

In the summer of 2015, The Sutton Trust, a charity whose focus is on improving social mobility through education, published *CHAIN EFFECTS 2015 – The Impact of Academy Chains on Low Income Students*. This was an update on a similar piece of work undertaken a year earlier. The studies set out to review how well disadvantaged pupils were achieving in academy chains based on 2014 exam results. The findings were that some chains continued to achieve impressive outcomes for their disadvantaged students against a range of measures, which indicated that they were helping to transform pupils' life chances. However, the report suggested that a larger group of low-performing chains was not having this effect and the results of disadvantaged students were not improving. Among its recommendations was one that Ofsted should be able to inspect chains as well as individual academies, and there are moves in this direction.

Some chains are a mixture of mainstream and special schools, others may only have mainstream schools and a few are composed of special schools. The Eden Academy is an example of a multi-academy trust of five special schools. John Ayres, the principal of Grangewood School and CEO of the MAT, explains that:

> The idea of creating an Academy of several schools grew out of a belief that schools working together and supporting each other is the best way to

achieve success. It means that we can share skills and experiences more widely. We can extend our social networks for our children and families and pool resources, providing them with a greater range of opportunities. (John Ayres, The Eden Academy [http://www.theedenacademy.co.uk/our-approach])

Case study

The Eden Academy

The five schools in the MAT are:

Alexandra School in Harrow is a multi-ethnic, multi-faith primary school for over 80 pupils aged 3–12 with a wide range of complex needs. Half the pupils have English as an additional language (EAL). The school has an outreach provision and offers training to local schools in: behaviour management, inclusion, working with children with autism, and planning and assessment for SEND pupils.

Grangewood School is a primary school in Eastcote, Middlesex for children with severe learning difficulties (SLD) and physical and complex needs, including ASD. Teaching takes place in different environments, including an interactive learning centre (ILC), a sensory room, hall, nature trail, sand room, spa and hydrotherapy pools.

Moorcroft School is a purpose-built secondary school based in Uxbridge, for young people with SLD. It also has a dedicated department for profound and multiple learning difficulties (PMLD) and a learning lodge for pupils with autism. The school employs two creative therapists and also uses Rebound therapy. There is a Signalong tutor to help with communication.

Pentland Field School is a new all-age special free school in Ickenham for pupils with MLD, SLD and ASD, between the ages of 5 and 19. It will ultimately provide 140 places across three phases: primary, secondary and post-16.

RNIB Sunshine House School is a school and children's home for blind and partially-sighted children who have significant learning difficulties and disabilities and are aged 3 to 14 years. It is based in Northwood, Middlesex and is a non-maintained special school (NMSS) run by the Royal National Association of Blind People (RNIB).

Having a group of different special schools working together in this way, provides unusual opportunities for staff development which can then be shared more widely with local mainstream schools.

Key information: Creative therapies and rebound therapy

Creative therapies include: art therapy, music therapy, dramatherapy and dance movement therapy. A further development is Cross Media & Mainstream Arts, where different therapists work together and link what they do with community arts and formal education. Further information on all of these therapies can be found at www.crea-tivetherapies.co.uk. It is based in Scotland.

Rebound therapy was founded in the UK in 1972. It is a specific model of exercise therapy, which uses trampolines to combine opportunities for movement, therapeutic exercise and recreation. Accredited and approved Rebound Therapy training courses are available. Details can be found at www.reboundtherapy.org

---

A variety of other partnerships

Multi-academy trusts and teaching school alliances are just two of the ways that groups of schools are working together. Former distinctive lines between the sectors have been further removed by schools working in partnership through federations, trusts, co-operatives and many other less formal arrangements. The co-location of mainstream and special schools provides significant opportunities for learning for the staff involved, as well as for the pupils. There were case studies in Chapter 2 of recently co-located schools. An earlier and particularly ambitious example of co-location was The Education Village in Darlington, and it is interesting to see how this has developed since the initial concept.

Opened in 2006 by Tony Blair, when he was prime minister, the village originally comprised:

- Springfield, a primary school of 200 pupils
- Beaumont Hill, a special school of about the same size, and
- Haughton, a 900-place secondary school.

The schools were not just on the same campus but designed as one building with different wings to accommodate each school, and many shared spaces were incorporated into the planning. Built round a village green used for community events and concerts, today The Education Village has become an Academy Trust which includes two more schools:

- Gurney Pease Academy, a primary school with a nursery, and
- Marchbank Free School, a 30-place provision for pupils who have BESD/SEMH.

Although not physically attached in the same way as the original three schools, they add to the range of personalised learning opportunities for pupils and the broadening of staff expertise.

The original concept for The Village came from Dela Smith when she was head of Beaumont Hill. From being the head teacher of this special school when it was a stand-alone entity, to seeing her vision of an Education Village realised, Dela led The Village until retiring from her post in December 2010. On her retirement, she said: 'The only regret I have is that the Education Village wasn't built ten years earlier. Children are children and they all deserve the same high-quality education. It is the most inclusive setting we could ever hope to come across and it's the right thing'.

A different kind of partnership is to be found in Northern Ireland, where four special schools have come together to share training days involving the whole staff of each school. While academies do not exist in the province, the same value is placed on working collaboratively. The schools have similar populations of mainly SLD and PMLD children, but with many other conditions as well, including autism and physical and mental health needs. A very brief synopsis of the schools is given in the case study.

Case study

Four special schools in Northern Ireland

There are 40 special schools in N. Ireland. The four in this case study are in the South of the province.

Donard School is a purpose-built school for 85 pupils aged 3 to 19 years. It is situated in Banbridge where it is located close to the Banbridge Campus of the Southern Regional College. This enables pupils at KS4 and KS5 to enrol in a variety of FE courses. A thematic approach is taken to the curriculum and the agreed cross-curricular topics are adapted to meet the needs of each individual.

Lisanally School, Armagh, has 3 departments: Early Years/Primary, Secondary Department, as well as a Vocational Training Unit for 16–19-year-olds. A range of accredited courses is offered from KS3 upwards and a programme to develop functional living skills enhances life opportunities. Involvement in the Armagh Area Learning Community has fostered close links with local schools. Sharing a campus with Southern Regional College, both engage in a Schools Partnership Programme.

(Continued)

(Continued)

Rathore School, Newry, is divided into three departments: Early Years and Primary, Secondary and Post-16. The latter department includes opportunities for work experience and involvement in the local community, as well as for participating in a link course with the Southern Regional College. The school has close links with several local schools and is an active member of the Newry and Mourne Area Learning Community.

Sperrinview School, Dungannon meets the needs of approximately 110 pupils aged 3–19 years. The school has been extended twice since opening in 1996. As well as multi-sensory and soft play areas inside, the school has a sensory garden, adventure playground and woodland classroom outside. There are strong links with nursery, primary and post-primary schools and with colleges in the area, and the South West College. These provide opportunities for extended learning, community involvement and working with a wider range of students.

Despite the differences in the way special schools are administered in England and in NI and the legal framework in which they operate, the way a continuum of provision is linking up shows many similarities. Special schools in NI are no more isolated from the community they serve than in this country. As in England, there are many links that are valuable to all concerned. In 2015, there was a Review of Special School Provision in NI (DENI 2015). While the Review made it clear that 'Special schools are an integral part of the education sector', there are concerns that they may become more generic, based on having a spread of special schools in each locality, rather than focusing on meeting different needs within the SEN continuum.

'Never give up on them and don't let them give up on themselves.'

Individual and flexible packages of support

The final examples in this chapter are of how different schools are providing individual packages of support to make sure every pupil feels included. Dawn Copping is the head teacher of Shaw Primary Academy in Ockendon, Thurrock. Like many schools, Dawn's has been involved with the Inclusion Quality Mark (IQM) and has now achieved Flagship School status.

Key Points: Inclusion Quality Mark (IQM)

The IQM is open to all kinds of schools, whether special or mainstream. The scheme provides an audit of what is happening in a school in terms of its journey towards inclusion.

Centre of Excellence is an award open to IQM schools who want to collaborate in sharing effective practice across a cluster of schools and engaging in classroom-level research activities.

Flagship School is a further award for IQM schools which have continued to sustain and develop their inclusive practice, including further research and disseminating it across a wider range of schools. They agree to an annual IQM visit and to create a yearly development plan (www.inclusionmark.co.uk).

There is a children's centre on the same site as the Shaw Academy, which is a single academy trust (SAT). The school is a strategic partner in the Dilkes Primary Teaching School Alliance. This consists of 17 primary schools – one of which also has teaching school status – and one special school.

Case study

Shaw Primary School's Pupil Jobs

This is a two-form entry school for 452 pupils aged 3–11. The Inclusion Team is led by an Inclusion Manager and consists of: a hands-on SENCO, a lead LSA for EAL and one for BESD. There is also an Inclusion Suite.

A special feature of the school is the Pupil Jobs on offer every term. There is a vacancy board in the entrance and pupils have to apply in writing and go through an interviewing process. Successful applicants are paid in house points and they can be removed from their post if their performance is unsatisfactory. Although all pupils can apply for these, they have proved a particularly valuable way of raising the self-esteem of vulnerable pupils, including some who have special needs.

For instance, a pupil who has cerebral palsy and is confined to a wheelchair has the job of keeping all the junior reading books correctly

(Continued)

(Continued)

organised and in the appropriate boxes. He checks the storage area and makes sure everything is arranged to make it easy for pupils to select the books they want. To enable him to carry out his role, the books have been placed at an appropriate height for him to be able to carry out the work from his wheelchair.

Another pupil, who is on the autism spectrum, has the highly prestigious role of Senior Monitor. These pupils have to exemplify what is expected by way of conduct as well as commitment to learning. In this girl's case, some simplified tasks have been devised, such as delivering messages and taking round the registers, so that she can take on the role at her own level. She does so without the presence of her one-to-one assistant, but has the support instead of one of her peers, who makes sure she is safe and happy. This is a great step on the road to independence for her.

Dawn says: 'Our philosophy is based on knowing and meeting the needs of all learners. Knowing what they "can" do is one thing, the secret is knowing what they "could" do. Once you know that everyone can achieve great things'.

Moving from a primary to a secondary school case study, Gareth Morewood is the SENCO and head of curriculum support at Priestnall School in Stockport. Although this is a large secondary school, he has the same individual approach to meeting pupils' needs. His attitude is not to wait until every piece of paper is in place but to 'crack on and find a solution'. As he points out, if pupils need help with overcoming a difficulty, they need it now, not when all the paperwork has been done. He says: 'Inclusion is at the heart of what we do. We have an ethos that, like the Every Child Matters (ECM) agenda, it is all about the individual'.

Case study

Priestnall School, Stockport

This is a larger than average secondary school, with double the average number of pupils who have statements/EHC plans, but it is below average for SEND. The school is designated as a centre for physical disabilities (PD). It has sports college status. The head teacher, John Cregg, is an NLE and the school is a National Support School (NSS).

To overcome its size, the school is divided into four colleges, which enables students' academic and pastoral needs to be met. The school has around 130 pupils eligible for free school meals (FSM) and about another 20 who receive the pupil premium because they are in the care system. The money is used for extra support leading up to exams, including: stress intervention; in-school counselling and therapy; mentoring; and running a nurture group. In addition, the school also uses the money to employ a trainee EP.

To move from a medical model to a more therapeutic one, Gareth's first appointment was that of a psychotherapist. More recently, the school has appointed its own speech and language therapist (SaLT) and an art therapist for 15-week interventions. The latter has been found to be particularly helpful for those who have suffered trauma or are on the autism spectrum, in helping them deal with the ups and downs of life. Gareth worked with an animal behaviourist to develop a project whereby pupils were able to bring their dogs into school. For one pupil, having dog training classes with his pet helped him to re-engage with learning, while pupils who were non-verbal became much more expressive.

Gareth involves students with SEND to help explain their difficulties to others. For instance, pupils with autism will take assemblies to help other pupils to understand their different view of the world. His individual support for students has included using different funding streams to allow a pupil with speech, language and communication needs (SLCN) to continue with the same SaLT when transferring to FE college. For another pupil whose difficult behaviour had caused him to be excluded many times from his primary school, Gareth tapped into different funding streams to provide him with a more personalised curriculum, including trips out, access to a Forest School, dramatherapy, and a key worker to support him and his family.

Gareth believes that if parents want their child to be in a mainstream setting, they have that right and it is his job to lead a team of staff who will do their best to make it possible. One parent expressed her gratitude by saying she just wanted her son to be happy and to be able to cope with moving on to college. She knew he had been at risk of permanent exclusion many times, but the school had not given up on him. The school's figure for NEETs (Not in Education, Employment or Training) has been zero for the last three years, which may be due, at least in part, to the school's very individualised approach.

'Children starved of love may appear less lovable.'

A bespoke curriculum

To complete this chapter and its emphasis on having provision for the whole range of needs and to use it in a flexible manner, the final case study is about children who need 24-hour provision for up to

52 weeks a year. As this provision is extremely specialist, and potentially expensive, it is rarely viable for LAs to maintain or create their own; instead, private companies are finding ways to provide it. One such is Specialist Education Services (SES) which was established by two very experienced heads of schools for children with severe social, emotional and mental health difficulties (SEMH schools – previously known as BESD schools), Jon Lees and Steve Lord. In 2005, they established Avocet House and in 2012 opened a further similar provision, Turnstone House. Jon says he prefers to talk about 'traumatised' children rather than 'damaged', because he believes they can be turned round, however unapproachable and unlovable they appear to be, provided they receive bespoke, specialised education and care.

Case study

Avocet House and Turnstone House, East Anglia

Both houses are dual registered as schools and as children's homes. Each caters for up to eight pupils between the ages of 8 and 18. All have a statement or an EHC plan, which usually identifies severe and complex SEMH (previously known as BESD). The majority are in care and reach these provisions only after going through a circuit of schools not being able to meet their complex needs, and so ultimately the current system failing them. This repeated failure to find support exacerbates their sense of rejection and failure as they are moved from one place to the next. Jon describes the population as a 'biomass of vulnerable children churning round in a tumble dryer'. SES has a strapline of 'A no limits approach to helping children', most of whom have experienced exclusion and rejection from a series of schools and social care placements. The usual route to the schools is via social care. The average length of stay is 3.4 years, with stays ranging from six months to over six years. Some pupils are able to settle down and achieve their GCSEs, and all are encouraged to believe in success not failure.

As their core need is for education *and* somewhere to live, the two cannot be separated. The approach is to provide a therapeutic environment involving multi-disciplinary, psychiatric and psychological support and a curriculum which starts from their personal interests. This is possible as much of the teaching is one-to-one, creating a suitable environment for children who have frequently been traumatised by abuse or neglect resulting in many issues, including those related to attachment. The schools are determined to work with the families, and create opportunities to do this systemically whenever possible. This might be with a parent or other family member, so some of the therapeutic approaches are for everyone concerned rather than just the pupil – a truly systemic approach. Taking this approach, the aim is to gradually re-introduce the child into the family setting if possible and, if not, prepare them for independent living.

The school's view of the eclectic, therapeutic approach it adopts is that it provides:

- A high quality physical environment
- The development of the interpersonal environment
- A chance to restore the excitement of learning
- Behavioural interventions, family work and individualised focused therapies, which are selected as a result of an assessment.

Each pupil has a personal tutor and a learning mentor, who, between them, take care of learning and relationships, as well as links with social workers and the family.

Jon says the volume and demand for high-quality holistic provision is high and there are many Looked After Children whose needs are not being met. This is put into perspective by considering that with an ongoing capacity for eight pupils, Avocet House has only admitted a total of 24 children in its ten-year history. There is thus a dichotomy between exhibiting such a success indicator in respect of stability of placement and permanence, and the limitations of their representing a drop in the ocean compared to the volume of need. He says that their vision statement intrinsically rejects the 'one size fits all' mentality and instead adopts an eclectic approach that puts the individual child at the centre. Such a setting may seem very expensive, but if it turns round the lives of these traumatised youngsters it must be a price worth paying.

Summary

This chapter has considered some of the ways that special schools have become embedded in the system, to be an integral part of a continuum of provision. Case studies illustrated the ways in which special schools are reaching out to other schools and settings, as well as offering more personalised programmes for their own pupils with complex needs.

The personalised approach taken across mainstream primary and secondary schools to meet the needs of their pupils was illustrated. The chapter closed with a case study where the needs of the young people are so great that they require a 24-hour bespoke curriculum in order to give them a chance to make a success of a life that has been fraught with adverse circumstances.

Further reading

DENI (2015) *Review of Special School Provision in Northern Ireland*. www.deni.gov.uk/publications/review-special-school-provision-northern-ireland

NCTL (2014) *Impact of Teaching Schools.* https://www.gov.uk/government/uploads/system/uploads/attachment_data/file/309938/teaching-schools-impact-report-2014.pdf

Sutton Trust (2015) *CHAIN EFFECTS 2015 – The Impact of Academy Chains on Low Income Students.* www.suttontrust.com

Tutt, R. (2012) *How Successful Schools Work: The Impact of Innovative Leadership*. London: Sage.

5

Meeting different needs more effectively

'Diversity is universal; we are all different.'

Chapter overview

This chapter considers the four broad categories of need identified in the SEND Code of Practice 2015. Following a reminder of these categories, there are additional sections on autism, behaviour, and on social, emotional and mental health needs (SEMH).

The chapter moves on to look at how the progress and achievements of pupils with SEND can be measured and how staff can become better trained to deal with the whole range of needs.

There are case studies of two schools for pupils with autism, another school that has had a particular role with assessment, and a free school for pupils with speech, language and communication needs (SLCN), which is part of a multi-academy trust (MAT) and on the same campus as the lead school in a teaching school alliance.

The SEND continuum

In the 2001 SEN Code of Practice, children and young people's needs were grouped under four broad headings:

1. Communication and interaction
2. Cognition and learning
3. Behaviour, emotional and social development (BESD)
4. Sensory and/or physical impairment.

In the SEND Code 2015, the only one that was changed was BESD, which became social, emotional and mental health needs (SEMH). The reason for this was that, instead of simply seeing some pupils' behaviour as a problem, it was better to look beneath the behaviour at what was causing it. So, the current headings cover the following:

1 Communication and interaction

This includes those who have speech, language and communication needs (SLCN) and those who are on the autism spectrum. Their difficulties may lie in one or more of the following areas:

*   Being able to communicate what they want to say (expressive skills)
*   Understanding what is said to them (receptive skills)
*   Understanding the social rules of communication.

Children with autism have particular difficulty with the last of these, ranging from those who say very little to those with Asperger's syndrome, where they may be happy to talk incessantly about their particular areas of interest, but fail to take on board whether the listener is interested in the subject. In other words, they have difficulty accepting that communication is a two-way process, in the same way that they may fail to grasp the two-way nature of friendship. Other children in this category include those whose language development is delayed and who may catch up in a richer language environment, and those whose language development is disordered in some way, in which case they are likely need the skilled help of a speech and language therapist (SALT). There is an example of a special free school for pupils with SLCN later in this chapter, which is part of a multi-academy trust (MAT) and teaching school alliance based on a mainstream secondary school.

Further information and resources, many of them free to download, are available from The Communication Trust (www.communicationtrust.org. uk) and from the Autism Education Trust (AET) (www.autismeducation trust.org.uk). The latter also has a large training programme, and by the summer of 2016 had trained over 100,000 professionals.

Two case studies of schools for pupils with autism are given further on in this chapter.

2 Cognition and learning

These are the pupils who learn at a slower pace than their peers in some or all areas of learning and many will have additional needs as well. It includes those who have

- Moderate learning difficulties (MLD)
- Severe learning difficulties (SLD)
- Profound and multiple learning difficulties (PMLD)
- Specific learning difficulties (SpLD).

The first three of these are pupils who will be slower in all areas of learning. At one time, the majority of pupils with MLD were in special schools. Now most of these pupils are educated in mainstream schools. Where MLD schools still exist, they are likely to include a wider range of pupils, for instance those who have MLD and additional difficulties, or other types of need. Pupils with SLD and PMLD are often educated together, but the main shift here has been the increasing proportion of pupils with PMLD, due, at least in part, to the rise in very premature births mentioned in Chapter 2 of this book. A charitable organisation in the UK that acts on behalf of children, young people and adults with SLD and PMLD is 'EQUALS'.

Key information: EQUALS

EQUALS has offered its services to schools, as well as to families, for over 20 years. It was formed in 1994 by a number of teachers, head teachers, parents, academics and activists in the field. It took on the role of writing schemes of work adapted to the needs of pupils and students with SLD and PMLD, in the wake of the National Curriculum, which became obligatory for all UK schools in 1988, yet with little attention being paid to its appropriateness for these groups of learners.

Since then, its work has extended to become a campaigning organisation, in addition to continuing being active in the area of curriculum development, including in relation to a toolkit for the 19–25 age group.

(www.equals.co.uk)

The other significant sub-section in cognition and learning is SpLD, where, unlike MLD, SLD or PMLD, only some areas of learning are affected. Three types are mentioned in the Code. The best known is dyslexia, which mainly affects reading and spelling. Increasing attention is being paid to dyscalculia, which results in an inability to understand basic number concepts or to comprehend quantitative and spatial information. Dyspraxia, also known as developmental co-ordination disorder (DCD), affects the person's ability to control the muscles involved in movement and balance. One that is not mentioned in the Code but is sometimes recognised is dysgraphia. Unlike dyslexia there is no difficulty with reading, but there is with writing, both the physical act of getting words down on paper and putting thoughts and ideas into a written form. Further information and resources are available from The Dyslexia-SpLD Trust at www.thedyslexia-spldtrust.org.uk. Both this trust and The Communication Trust have a large number of interventions that have been well researched and are useful if a child is not making progress and a different intervention needs to be explored.

3 Social, emotional & mental health needs (SEMH)

This is the one category that has changed from the 2001 Code. As well as the need to look behind a child's behaviour to what is causing it, the title was changed to reflect the increasing attention being given to pupils who have mental health conditions. Although it is recognised that children and young people with SEND are more prone to develop mental health issues, it is also the case that they may be harder to spot, as the presenting need may make the mental health need less obvious and both parents and professionals may put the symptoms down to the child's special needs rather than thinking this could be a co-existing condition. In society at large, there has been a belated recognition that much less attention is paid to a person's mental health than their physical well-being. This is very evident in the far larger amount of money spent on physical than on mental health.

The Code explains that children and young people who experience social and emotional difficulties range from the very withdrawn and isolated child, to the ones exhibiting challenging, disruptive or disturbing behaviour, and that either of these behaviours may be due to underlying mental health problems. When the Code first introduced this term, teachers were divided between those who were worried by the idea that schools should have anything to do with mental health, and those who were pleased that, at last, its significance had been recognised. Although the majority of staff in early years settings, schools and colleges, will not be trained in mental health, a great deal can be learned through observation, particularly if staff have some idea of what to look out for. There is further discussion on these matters after the section on autism, at which point there are pointers to sources of further support and advice.

4 Sensory and/or physical needs

In relation to sensory needs, this generally refers to:

- Hearing impairment (HI)
- Visual impairment (VI)
- Multi-sensory impairment (MSI).

Both hearing impairment and visual impairment are further divided depending on the severity of the condition. Hearing impairment includes profound deafness, while visual impairment includes those who are blind.

Children and young people with MSI have a combination of vision and hearing difficulties. As these are low-incidence needs, most LAs will rely on having provision in the form of units attached to mainstream schools. They may also have a sensory impairment team, whereby teachers of the deaf and/or visually impaired are able to provide support for pupils and their teachers. There are also a few special schools for HI and VI. Profoundly deaf pupils may need to learn through a total communication approach that includes signing. Those registered blind may need to be taught to use Braille or a simplified version called 'Moon'. Further information about sensory impairments is available on the following websites:

Royal National Institute of Blind People (RNIB): www.rnib.org.uk

National Deaf Children's Society (NDCS): www.ndcs.org.uk

Sense is the organisation for deafblind people (or MSI): www.sense.org.uk

Physical impairments are, perhaps, better understood as the difficulties are more visible, but this does not make the barriers to learning easy to overcome. Again, there is a huge variation, which ranges from limitations in being able to sit, stand and walk, to those who are wheelchair users and rely on systems of augmentative and alternative communication (AAC). For further details visit Scope (renamed 20 years ago from 'The Spastics Society') at: www.scope.org.uk

---

Questions for reflection

Do you think the idea of having four broad categories are helpful? What are the advantages and disadvantages of this approach?

What do you think about the change from BESD to SEMH? Do you think it will make a difference? If so, will it be a change for the better?

As the word 'behaviour' is no longer mentioned, do you see this as an attempt to gloss over behavioural difficulties in educational settings or a way to look at behaviour in a more constructive way?

'I don't want to be 'cured' of autism; I want to be understood.'

Autism

Although this has already been touched on under the general heading of 'communication and interaction' it has become one of the areas of increasing concern, not least because provision has found it hard to keep up with demand. It is often thought of as a triad of impairments:

1. Social communication – including a lack of understanding of how people communicate through gesture, facial expression and tone of voice as well as through words
2. Social interaction – including not understanding social rules or the interaction involved in friendships
3. Social imagination – including not knowing how to interpret people's thoughts and feelings or to predict what might happen next.

More recently, two other elements have been given greater prominence as well. These are:

*   Difficulties with sensory processing, resulting in being hyper- or hypo-sensitive, or finding it hard to integrate information coming through different senses at the same time, causing overload and sometimes 'meltdowns'
*   Having special interests or obsessions, enabling the person to focus intensely on a very narrow range of activities, which may or may not be productive.

While the majority of those on the autism spectrum will cope with being in a mainstream environment, they are likely to need a level of under-standing from staff about the different ways they experience the world, so adjustments can be made to the setting to make it less stressful. A minority of children and young people will need an environment that is geared specifically to helping them to learn. Some of these children will also have significant learning difficulties, while others, despite having good aca-demic potential, will still need a more specialist setting due to their high levels of anxiety.

The next two case studies illustrate two different schools for pupils on the autism spectrum. The first example is a school run by the National Autistic Society (NAS). There are eight NAS schools to date, two in Scotland and six in England. One of the schools in England is a free school, with another NAS free school due to open in Essex in 2017. All the schools use the NAS SPELL philosophy based on:

Structure (to reduce anxiety resulting from rigidity of thought)

Positivity (recognising autistic intelligence to enhance self-esteem)

Empathy (seeking to recognise the perspective of the person with autism)

Low arousal (to reduce anxiety related to sensory differences)

Links (to other interventions and to the wider community).

However, elements of other approaches are used as well. Jo Galloway, the head teacher in the first case study, Radlett Lodge, stresses the importance of making each pupil feel a sense of belonging to the school and being part of the community. A personalised approach to the curriculum is taken which recognises the child's strengths and interests.

Case study

Radlett Lodge, Hertfordshire

This school in Radlett is purpose-built to cater for 55 pupils from 4 to 19. It has residential accommodation for 14 weekly or termly boarders, which is in a separate house on the same site. The school is all-age and divided into:

Early years, when the curriculum is based on the Early Years Foundation Stage (EYFS) framework, together with the school's Learning to Learn Curriculum which focuses on important life skills and readiness to learn.

Primary and Secondary, which are based on a differentiated national curriculum, with a strong emphasis on communication and PSHCE (personal, social, health and citizenship education) in all lessons.

A Post-16 Unit for 12 pupils who prefer to stay on rather than transfer elsewhere. Each student has a personalised programme drawn from:

- Functional skills in English, Maths and ICT
- Vocational skills, such as horticulture and business enterprise
- Work experience and work placements
- Personal and social development
- Leisure, sport, health and wellbeing.

The programme takes place at the school, in the community and at local colleges. The attitude of the staff is not to be too precise about what is on offer, as they believe in offering what the students need. The school has strong links with several colleges in the area as well as a range of other providers.

The school offers flexi-boarding alongside its other boarding provision. This includes overnight stays and activity day schemes with residence over weekends or holidays.

There is a programme of continuous professional development for staff (CPD), to which the staff of local schools are invited. In addition, staff visit other schools to deliver training on topics such as: autism awareness, behaviour management, sensory issues, communication and self-injurious behaviour.

Whereas Radlett Lodge accepts both boys and girls with a wide ability range and other complex needs, the next school is only for girls on the autism spectrum, most of whom are in the average ability range. Recently, an increasing interest has been taken nationally in whether there really are far fewer girls with autism, or whether it is because they are less likely to be diagnosed. It appears that some may get by until their teens and then are diagnosed with anxiety or eating disorders, or they are picked up because they are self-harming, rather than the underlying cause being considered.

Case study

Limpsfield Grange, Oxted

This is a community special school for around 70 girls between the ages of 11 and 16, with 24 places for boarders. They come from Surrey and a wide range of LAs across the country. Most have a diagnosis of autism, but some have other communication and interaction difficulties. Many of the students who attend Limpsfield Grange have persistent and debilitating levels of anxiety, speech, language and communication difficulties or other additional disorders.

Students are disapplied from learning another language, so the time can be spent on improving their communication skills in English. At key stage 4, they take GCSE courses or Entry Level certificates.

The residential students benefit from a Rainbow Curriculum, which is described as a journey through life skills that promotes self-esteem, resilience and independence. It covers: personal care; understanding me; community and social interaction; practical living skills; and travel and public transport.

The school makes a point of encouraging pupils to talk to people and, as they get older, some have the confidence and insight into their own circumstances to be able to tell groups of adults what it means to them to have autism. For instance, one described knowing she was different before she came to the school, but not knowing why. She said: 'I tried to fit in but I didn't know how. Now I'm not afraid to be who I am. Sometimes my stomach twists and I start shaking without feeling anxious knowingly but music helps me calm down. I can't talk about emotions, but I can write them down.' She said she would like to study biomedical science or engineering, 'but I would like someone to help organise me and support me'.

Another girl explained how she copes with her anxiety: 'I go to a little world in my head when I'm anxious, but it has to come out somewhere or I explode. So I punch a pillow or draw the face of an enemy'. She went on to say: 'In mainstream I had to be different from myself. At the Grange I can be me. What is normal when everyone's different – which makes us all the same?'

Sarah Wild, the head teacher, says she sees special schools as a vital part of a flexible, needs-led continuum of provision: 'Some children and young people are unable to access mainstream provision due to their high and debilitating levels of social anxiety; their life-long mental health difficulties or their inability to cope with and process the sensory overload that a mainstream school can induce. Without access to the right provision they will not make the academic progress, or develop the appropriate social or independence skills that they will need to be economically viable, contented adults who can make a positive contribution to their local communities and society at large. Special schools can, and do, enable these wonderfully complex young people to reach their potential, thrive, and shine'.

'Look beneath, behind and beyond the behaviour.'

Behaviour

As mentioned earlier in this chapter, BESD is the one broad area of need that has changed from the 2001 Code of Practice. There is now an expectation that teachers will think about *why* a child may be behaving in a way that is causing concern. One reason may be that there are underlying mental health issues, and this will be discussed in the next section. The Code points out that 'Persistent or withdrawn behaviours do not necessarily mean that a child or young person has SEN', although, again, that needs to be considered as a possibility.

School behaviour expert

In June 2015, the government announced that Tom Bennett (variously described as a former Soho nightclub bouncer and as the current director of ResearchED [www.workingoutwhatworks.com]) would be appointed as a behaviour expert, to focus on the low-level disruption that stops pupils from learning. On taking up the position, Tom, who has, in fact, taught for many years, said:

Behaviour has been the elephant in the classroom for too long, and the amount of learning time lost because of disruption is a tragedy. At present, training teachers to anticipate, deal with and respond to misbehaviour is far too hit and miss … I'm delighted to lead a group which will offer advice on doing just that.

Tom prefers to talk about misbehaviour, rather than bad behaviour. He defines the former as being anything that acts as a barrier to learning. He recognises that newcomers to teaching may find it hard to set the firm boundaries as to what is and is not acceptable behaviour. He goes on to explain that:

> Many new teachers start off wanting to be really kind and friendly to their pupils. They believe they will win them over with the power of love ... They find that their ambitions are dashed against the cliffs of indifference to their eventual ruin, because children don't want, or need, a tall friend.

He also warns against too much group work, as it can be a situation that propagates misbehaviour.

Soon after he was appointed, Tom, who has been a regular columnist in the *Times Educational Supplement (TES)*, based one contribution on his top ten tips for maintaining classroom discipline. In short, they are:

1. Set out your behaviour expectations from the moment you meet your students.
2. Have a seating plan.
3. Know pupils' names.
4. If pupils break the rules, they have to pay the penalty.
5. Keep it up.
6. Don't walk alone.
7. Get the parents involved.
8. Don't freak out.
9. Be prepared.
10. Be their teacher, not their chum.

Supporting behaviour

Some schools have taken on the nurture group approach, an idea that was started by an educational psychologist, Marjorie Boxall, mainly for young children who had missed out on a nurturing environment at home. Today Nurture Groups can be found across the age range, in mainstream and in special schools. Sharon Gray, who had been head of several BESD schools before taking on the headship of a mainstream primary school, makes it clear that this arrangement should not be seen as a place to put children when they are playing up in class. She refers to them as not the children who are naughty, but the ones who:

- are withdrawn, unresponsive and have underdeveloped social skills
- have a poor concentration span and are developmentally behind their chronological age
- behave aggressively, impulsively or in ways that damage their ability to access and engage with the curriculum and with their peers

- find change challenging or upsetting
- appear unable to integrate into a mainstream classroom
- are emotionally insecure and have low self-worth or a lack of trust.

The Boxall Profile is a resource to help teachers understand emotional and social difficulties and to plan and track their progress (www.nurturegroups. org and www.boxallprofile.org).

As well as creating nurture groups, Sharon managed to have areas in each class where children could retreat into their own space when they needed time away from the group. Instead of *Behaviour Management*, the school developed an *Engagement and Mood Management Policy*, based on the key aims of: Restitution not Retribution; Reconciliation not Revenge; Rights and Respect.

Activity

Either on your own or with colleagues, try to find out more about the nurture group approach by:

- Researching the theories behind it
- Visiting settings that run nurture groups or use elements of this approach in other ways.

Then, discuss with colleagues:

1. What you see as the usefulness of this approach
2. Whether it can be equally useful in early years, primary, secondary and special school settings
3. Whether it is only valuable if used to create a nurture group (where young learners are together for much of the day), or whether it is equally valid to use elements of Boxall's method in normal classes.

Mental health and wellbeing

As far as the mental health of children and young people is concerned, 2015 was a year when education began to focus more fully on the matter. As well as a new Code of Practice appearing at the beginning of the year, in March 2015, four additional relevant documents were published. The DfE (2015f) brought out *Mental Health and Behaviour in Schools: Departmental Advice for School Staff*, which was updated in March 2016. (DfE 2016b) Although mental health conditions are a medical diagnosis, schools should be aware of, and record, changes in behaviour. Observation is a key factor in profiling mental health needs. The document includes a link to the *Strengths & Difficulties Questionnaire* (SDQ) (www.sdqinfo. com). This has scales to help identify: emotional symptoms; conduct problems; hyperactivity/inattention; peer relationship problems; and prosocial behaviour.

Also in March 2015, and published jointly by the Department of Health (DoH) & NHS England, *Future in Mind: Promoting, Protecting and Improving Children and Young People's Mental Health and Wellbeing* appeared. Alongside this report, two other documents were published. The first was the DfE's (2015b) *Counselling in Schools: A Blueprint for the Future – Departmental Advice for School Leaders and Counsellors*. The British Association of Counselling and Psychotherapists (BACP) keeps a register of professionals (www.bacp.co.uk).

The other document was *Teacher Guidance: Preparing to Teach about Mental Health and Emotional Wellbeing*. This has been produced by the PSHE Association (2015) with funding from the DfE. Detailed programmes are set out for KS1 to KS4.

A Mental Health Champion for Schools

In August 2015, the government appointed Natasha Devon as its first Mental Health Champion for Schools. In her teens, Natasha overcame an eating disorder and is keenly aware of the need to boost vulnerable pupils' self-esteem. When asked by a Tory government to take on this role, Natasha expressed her surprise, describing herself as a 'left-leaning "gob on a stick"'. By this time, she had already established two organisations: the Self-Esteem Team (www.selfesteemteam.org), which has been running workshops for pupils from Year 9 upwards, and Body Gossip (www.bodygossip.org), which campaigns through arts and education for a healthier and more realistic attitude towards physical appearance. They have also combined to create the Body Gossip Education Programme for 13–18-year-olds. Natasha has set out her Mental Health Manifesto under four headings:

1. A Teachers' Toolkit, providing a series of ten-minute exercises to improve mental and physical wellbeing
2. Compulsory mental health training for school nurses
3. Guidelines on DON'Ts for lessons on mental health, so that pupils are left feeling positive and empowered rather than negative and destructive
4. A mental health 'five a day', similar to advice on physical health, but involving switching off smart phones for two hours a day and having ten minutes for quiet reflection.

Having a Mental Health Champion seemed to be one of the many ways that the importance of mental health was, belatedly, being recognised. However, a few months into the role, Natasha was asked to step aside. The DfE said this was not because she had been outspoken about the dangers of too much testing on pupils' mental health, but because the government wished to create a cross-government mental health champion instead. Be that as it may, there will continue to be a need for mental health issues to be discussed as openly as physical health: 'One in ten children and young people have asthma. How is it that we "forget" that one in ten children and young people suffer from a diagnosable mental health disorder? Probably because it is far too taboo to talk about our mental health' (Anna Hicks, May 2015, http://www.huffingtonpost.co.uk/anna-hicks/mental-health_b_7268330.html).

Measuring progress

Turning now from looking at different types of need, the rest of the chapter is concerned with measuring the progress of pupils with SEND and how to have better trained staff.

Although measuring young learners' performance through national curriculum levels was a far from ideal approach, after becoming used to assessing children in this way over the course of 25 years, to have them abandoned without any certainty of what would replace them, caused some confusion. The schools minister referred to the data created by levels in the following terms: 'We had a system swimming in defective data on attainment and failed to see that our legal commitment to giving all children access to all of the national curriculum had been compromised'.

To help fill the vacuum created by the disappearance of levels, in May 2014 eight schools representing a cross-section of ages, phases and sectors were given money from the Assessment Innovation Fund to develop the materials they had put forward in their bids, and to make them accessible to all schools. One of the special schools chosen was Frank Wise in Oxfordshire.

Case study

Frank Wise School, Banbury

This is a school for over 100 pupils aged 2–16 years who have severe or profound and multiple learning difficulties (SLD and PMLD). The school decided to build on its well-established curriculum framework for

(Continued)

(Continued)

teaching Intellectual and Reasoning skills and the set of assessments which had been developed in-house to support this.

Using the Fund, the school refined a series of assessments that screen the level of development of basic cognitive skills, and created video and other training materials with a view to enabling teachers in other settings to establish a baseline and allowing them to plan appropriately challenging targets for future learning.

The framework for teaching Intellectual and Reasoning skills is set out on one page of a 40-page document, showing how a child's progress can be mapped through play and stimulation of the senses, to the development of early reasoning skills and then to the conceptual and reasoning skills of being able to categorise, to sequence and to memorise. On the following pages of the booklet, there are full explanations of all the stages of development. Through this approach, children's development can be tracked as well as where there are gaps in a child's progress and understanding.

Although these assessment materials were developed with SLD and PMLD children, the school worked closely with local schools on their development and they were found to be useful for some children in early years and local school settings.

Simon Knight, the deputy head of Frank Wise, who led the project, said: 'This will provide an opportunity for more children to have their individual needs identified more quickly, without necessarily waiting for the symptomatic indicators of delayed development to become apparent'. The materials are available from the school at www.frankwise.oxon. sch.uk and from iTunes at https://itunes.apple.com/gb/book/assessing-intellectual-reasoning/id1037393887?mt=11

A Commission on Assessment

In 2015, a Commission was established under the chairmanship of John McIntosh, to help schools develop and implement new approaches to pupil assessment. His report, *Commission on Assessment Without Levels: Final Report* (DfE 2015g), was published in September 2015. From summer 2016, results at KS1 and KS2, instead of being reported in levels, have been given a scaled score, with 100 representing the standard at each stage. For the end of KS4, a 'Progress 8' measure is being used based on results in GCSE exams, which is designed to track the progress a child makes between KS2 and KS4.

An Assessment Review

In July 2015, the DfE announced a *Review into Assessment of Pupils with Lower Attainment*, chaired by Diane Rochford, a special school head teacher.

A DfE press release at the time reckoned there were 50,000 pupils whose ability fell below the standard required to take national curriculum tests. The Rochford Review (DfE 2015h) looked first at the pupils who fell into the gap between the top end of the P scales (used by all schools to measure the progress of those at the lowest end of the ability range) and the standard required for statutory testing. In December 2015, the Rochford Review published three documents:

- *Statement on the Interim Recommendations of the Rochford Review*
- *Pre-Key Stage 1: Pupils Working below the Test Standard*
- *Pre-key Stage 2: Pupils Working below the Test Standard.*

A further piece of work was to consider whether the P scales should remain the same, be adjusted, or be abolished. A consultation took place and a final report was due out in the summer of 2016.

Scotland and assessment

Scotland's 'Curriculum for Excellence' was brought in over a number of years. It aims to deliver a personalised educational experience for every pupil. In September 2015, the Scottish Government released a draft National Improvement Framework, setting out the actions it proposes to take in order to close the attainment gap. Part of this will be to introduce National Standardised Assessments at four different stages of a child's education between 5 and 15 years of age. As Greg Dempster, the general secretary of the Association of Headteachers and Deputes in Scotland (AHDS), has pointed out, if this happens, it would compromise the core elements of the new curriculum which was designed to value breadth and to be personalised to the needs and interests of every pupil.

> *'Teaching is a craft that flows from a deep understanding of learning.'*

Teacher training

Knowing how to assess pupil progress was also a feature of *The Carter Review of Initial Teacher Training (ITT)*, which was published in January 2015 together with the DfE's response (DfE 2015d, 2015e). The first of Andrew Carter's 18 recommendations was that, with so many routes into ITT, it was necessary to have a framework of core content. The review suggested this should include:

- subject knowledge
- pupil assessment
- behaviour management
- special educational needs.

Currently, there is work going on to develop the core content and the SEND component within it.

Teaching school alliances

Teaching schools and their alliances were mentioned in the previous chapter, together with a case study of a large teaching school alliance, and today a large percentage of trainee teachers receive school-based training. Whereas the lead school in the Forest Way Teaching School Alliance (see Chapter 4) was a special school, the Suffolk Borders Teaching Alliance is led by the Samuel Ward Academy Trust (SWAT), which includes: four secondary schools, three primary schools and one special free school. The latter is Churchill School in Suffolk.

Case study

Churchill School, Haverhill

This is a special free school for up to 70 pupils aged 8–18 who have speech, language and interaction difficulties. This includes both those with SLCN and those on the autism spectrum. The children who attend are mostly from Suffolk, Cambridgeshire and Essex.

The school opened in September 2013 as part of SWAT and is housed in an adjacent building to the lead school, the Samuel Ward Academy. Over two-thirds of the pupils take some of their lessons there, which is made easier by both schools having the same timetable and curriculum.

The school is based on the belief that communication is a fundamental skill underpinning a child's social, emotional and educational development. The school's speech and language therapist (SaLT) works with parents and staff to provide one-to-one and small group work, as well as making sure that the whole environment is conducive to developing the pupils' communication skills to the full. The paediatric occupational therapist helps pupils who are assessed as needing support with motor skills and developing independence, so that they can do more for themselves rather than having to rely on others. The building has a number of calming rooms as well as a sensory room.

The school offers up to 15 places to pupils who do not yet have a statement or EHC plan. These pupils will either be undergoing assessment, or they are seen as likely to benefit from a period of short-term, intensive support, in order to catch up with their literacy and communication skills.

Summary

After identifying the four broad areas of need in the SEND Code of Practice and providing links to some of the main organisations concerned, the chapter went on to look in more depth at autism, behaviour and mental health needs.

The debates around the assessment of pupils with SEND and the need to train teachers, both to assess in a world where levels have disappeared and to have a thorough understanding of pupils with SEND, were explored, as was the question of how to improve ITT in the area of SEND.

The final case study of a special free school for pupils with SLCN showed the advantages of not only sharing a site with a mainstream secondary school, but having a matching curriculum and timetable to maximise a two-way flow of pupils.

Further reading

Bennett, T. (2015) *Managing Difficult Behaviour in Schools: A Practical Guide*. London: Unison. https://www.unison.org.uk/content/uploads/2015/04/On-line-Catalogue 22970.pdf

Dittrich, W.H. and Tutt, R. (2008) *Educating Children with Complex Conditions: Understanding Overlapping and Co-existing Developmental Disorders*. London: Sage.

DoH & NHS England (2015) *Future in Mind: Promoting, Protecting and Improving Children and Young People's Mental Health and Wellbeing*. https://www.gov.uk/government/uploads/system/uploads/attachment_data/file/414024/Childrens_Mental_Health.pdf

Martin, V. and students of Limpsfield Grange (2015) *M is for Autism*. London: Jessica Kingsley.

6

Beyond the inclusion debate

'Difficulties should identify strategies not barriers.'

Chapter overview

This chapter takes up the theme of having a broad continuum of provision by looking at what this means:

- At local authority (LA) level
- At a national level, using a different country from outside the UK and Europe as a point of comparison.

In many ways, the two LAs are a contrast, but what they have in common is that they have sought in different ways to achieve a continuum of provision that fits in with their history, their community and the wishes of the families they serve.

The chapter ends with a summary of where SEND is at the present time, before the final chapter explores where it might go from here.

A change of culture at the top

By 2018, we may have some idea of how far the SEND Reforms have improved practice and therefore the outcomes for children and young people. But there are several things that need to happen to secure the improvements and these are at national level, local level, and at the level of each educational establishment and setting.

The government has been very keen to stress that the SEND Reforms require a change of culture and a more personalised approach to young learners and their families. However, this is somewhat at variance with successive governments' desire to impose a curriculum on schools, together with a testing regime that assumes children and young people are much the same. The fixation on age not developmental stage and a narrow approach to measuring the success of schools, is at odds with taking a more individual approach to children and young people with SEND and those who belong to other vulnerable groups. Nor does any government in the last two decades seem concerned about the messages given out by the terminology of 'reaching the expected level' (when the expectation should be that all children are different), or 'working below the standard of the national curriculum', which, if it were a national curriculum, all young learners would be able to access. Despite these difficulties, and an era of significant financial restraint, LAs, and the partners they work with, have often been doing their best to make the reforms work, so that they improve the experience of children, young people and their families, and lead to better outcomes for them. The two examples that follow are of the London Borough of Newham and the North East Council of North Tyneside.

Newham

Since the 1980s, Newham has been at the forefront of the move to make schools more inclusive. During the 1990s, there was a commitment to improve access to mainstream schools which led to the closure of a number of special schools. Between 1990 and 2010, there was a concerted effort to support head teachers in improving provision for pupils with SEND in mainstream schools. In 2011, the LA undertook a significant review of its provision, given that the child population in Newham had risen significantly and arrangements to meet the needs of children with complex SEND seemed to be more challenging. As a result, Newham committed to developing a flexible offer to meet the needs of children with SEND. This included continuing to develop the offer for mainstream schools, expand resourced provision and ensure that special schools were included in the Local Offer.

The LA places high importance on engaging parents in discussions about developing provision in school and has a mandate from members, parents and the community to maximise the availability of local education for pupils with SEND. The strategic aim is to provide greater choice for families whose children have very complex needs.

Case study

Newham's approach to inclusion

The London Borough of Newham has around 100 schools and strong support so that children with SEND are able to access local provision. In 2015, this led to 2.4% of the school population having high needs funding, including the 0.8% of the school population who have statements or EHC plans.

James Hourigan, Newham's Head of Inclusion, says the LA's approach is to try to maximise the availability of local provision for every child, as most parents of children with SEND want their children in local schools. Key elements in providing for pupils in their local schools include maintaining a quality assurance function of the arrangements for SEND in schools and an offer to *all* schools that include strong advisory and support services and a commitment to targeted support for SENCOs and Inclusion Managers. Alongside this, Newham works with its schools to fund projects to increase the capacity of schools to meet the needs of pupils with SEND, including conferences, targeted programmes to support vulnerable groups and projects such as SCERTS (Social Communication, Emotional Regulation and Transactional Support).

With the emphasis over the last 15 years on making every school accessible, many of the resources usually found in special schools are in mainstream schools as well. These include:

- Strong links with capital investment projects to ensure that schools have lifts, wide doors and extended corridors to take wheelchairs
- The installation of accessible toilets and hygiene rooms
- The installation of sensory rooms or sensory spaces and soft play areas
- The employment of specialist and highly trained staff in schools
- Safe outdoor learning spaces.

If a school does not have the facilities to meet a child's individual needs, schools either use community resources or other facilities, such as climbing walls and hydrotherapy pools.

As a result, the LA has made significant investment in capital projects for both special schools and its mainstream schools with resourced provision. In 2011, there were 14 resourced provisions and this number is expected to increase to 22 by 2019. This includes the development of an all-age specialist provision run by Tollgate School, which is an outstanding mainstream school with an international reputation for inclusion.

The two special schools are:

John F. Kennedy, which is part of the Learning in Harmony Multi-Academy Trust (MAT). This brings together mainstream schools and the J.F. Kennedy special school academy. The school caters for 110 pupils aged 5–16, with severe learning difficulties (SLD), profound and multiple learning difficulties (PMLD), and autism across two sites.

Eleanor Smith is a specialist setting for children who have social and emotional needs. It caters for 80 pupils aged 5–16, most of whom have a link place in a mainstream school. The school promotes a model of early intervention.

The close links between the special schools and their local schools mean that there are plenty of opportunities for pupils to have the benefit of learning in both mainstream and specialist environments.

SCERTS autism training in Newham

An example of the way in which all schools are equipped to educate a very wide range of needs is the training the LA initiated for understanding autism using the SCERTS approach (www.scerts.com). This covered not just schools, but families and other agencies, in order to build capacity and embed expertise across the borough. The LA is well on its way to ensuring all its schools receive *Foundation Level* training, some go on to *Advanced Level* and others are pursuing *Flagship Level*. Response to the training has been very positive, with feedback from the parents attending including the following comments:

'I needed to share experiences with other parents to learn from them also. They make me feel we are a normal family.'

'It's motivating seeing other people in the same position as you and dealing with it bravely.'

'I met new people, exchanged experiences and learnt new strategies.'

'Light bulb moment of why Y. displays certain behaviours.'

'Thank you – I've been waiting for these sessions but just didn't know it.'

And the following comments were made by some of the attending school staff:

'Staff are now able to use a "consistent" language to describe a student's behaviour.'

'Emotional Regulation targets have reduced challenging behaviour.'

'This was one of the most informative courses I have attended, with strategies to take back to my school and implement.'

'It led to a more focused relationship with families.'

Newham's policy, which was updated in line with the Children and Families Act 2014, states that children and young people should receive:

- the right support
- in the right place
- for the right things
- at the right time.

Newham's approach to inclusion is an example of how a range of provision can be used flexibly according to pupils' needs. This might be summarised as follows:

Mainstream   Resourced mainstream   Special schools with mainstream links

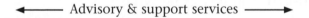

◄──────── Advisory & support services ──────►

North Tyneside

The Metropolitan Borough of North Tyneside came into being in April 1974. It is an area of considerable diversity, as it includes deprived neighbourhoods and more affluent ones. North Tyneside Council is the local government authority for the Metropolitan Borough. It does not include Newcastle and its main towns are Wallsend, North Shields and Whitley Bay. There are 77 schools:

- 1 nursery school
- 56 primary schools, including 8 first schools
- 15 secondary schools, including 4 middle schools
- 5 special schools

and 2 pupil referral units (PRUs).

The majority of schools, including the five special schools, have joined the North Tyneside Learning Trust, which is a collaboration of schools working with employers, universities and colleges. It includes the school improvement service.

Case study

North Tyneside's approach to inclusion

In addition to its five special schools, the borough has a number of mainstream schools described as having Additionally Resourced Provision (ARP). This includes:

- an ARP nursery attached to a first school
- 9 ARPs for moderate learning difficulties (MLD): 4 primary and 5 secondary
- a primary and 2 secondary ARPs for speech, language & communication needs (SLCN)
- a primary and a secondary ARP for physical disability (PD)
- 2 primary and 1 secondary ARP for hearing impairment (HI).

The LA has a number of educational support services. As well as the Education Psychology Service (EPS) and the Education Welfare Service (EWS), there are the following:

- Sensory Support Team
- Language & Communication Team
- Dyslexia Referral Team
- Portage
- SEN School Improvement Advisory Team
- Senior Adviser SEN
- SEN Teaching & Support Service.

In addition, the schools with Additionally Resourced Provision and the special schools also provide support for other schools through outreach and consultancy work.

Special schools

The special schools include:

Beacon Hill in Wallsend is for 2–19-year-olds who have SLD and PMLD. The school has a specialism in Business and Enterprise. Its post-16 provision is at Queen Alexandra Specialist College. The school manages the LA's portage and sensory support services.

Benton Dene School in Longbenton is for 5–11-year-olds with MLD and/or autism. The school is co-located in a new building with Benton Dene Primary School to form an integrated primary learning campus.

The LA's language and communication team is based at the Dene Communication Centre, which is a specialist nursery situated within the special school.

Silverdale School in Wallsend for 7–16-year-olds caters for pupils with emotional, social and behavioural difficulties (ESBD). Silverdale has an additional provision for primary-aged pupils who are admitted on assessment places. The school uses three types of alternative provision in order to provide different options and courses to re-engage pupils.

Southlands School in North Shields is for 11–16-year-olds with MLD, SEBD, or other needs. An on-site provision called EPICC (Extended provision for the inclusion of challenging children) is available as an alternative for those who need time away from the main classes.

Woodlawn School in Whitley Bay is for 2–19-year-olds with a range of complex difficulties, including physical, medical and sensory needs. It has an assessment unit within its early years provision and a wide range of post-16 courses. There is a large multi-disciplinary team on the same site.

Working together across the continuum

One of the teaching school alliances in the area is the *Shine Teaching School Alliance*, whose lead school is Shiremoor Primary School. This is a partnership of schools and institutions sharing skills, experience, talent and capacity to help improve learning and achievement in schools across North Tyneside and the surrounding area.

Case study

Shine Teaching School Alliance

The Alliance is led by Barbara Slider, who is a local leader of education (LLE) and head teacher at Shiremoor Primary School. The school's slogan is: *Our mission is to work together to provide world class teaching and learning so that every single one of our students and teachers get to shine.*

Fourteen schools make up the Alliance Partnership and between them they cover the age range from the early years upwards. Northumbria University and The University of Nottingham are the universities involved. The Alliance has been running the School Direct programme for three years with successful trainee teachers gaining the PGCE in Education with QTS (qualified teacher status).

As outlined in Chapter 4 of this book, initial teacher training (ITT) is only one of the six aspects which must be covered by all teaching schools. Another is to be a source of continuing professional development (CPD). An example of how teaching school alliances encourage schools to work in partnership with each other and with other organisations, was a SEND conference which the Alliance put together in the autumn of 2015. This entailed close working between Shine, three of the special schools who were involved in the planning and delivered workshops on the day, and the LA, whose advisory and support services ran further workshops.

At the conference, those present were asked to write their definition of inclusion, either specifically with SEND children and young people in mind, or taking a broader view. This produced considerable agreement about the nature of inclusion. These are some of the ideas that were put forward:

Inclusion means ...

- Everyone valued
- Being fully accepted for who you are
- A focus on the whole child
- Everyone's needs being met
- Equal access to learning for all
- The majority changing what they do for the sake of the minority
- Removing any or all of the barriers that exclude
- Collaborative decision making by families and children
- Taking account of the child's and family's needs
- Benefiting all children, learning to be tolerant and understanding of others
- Allowing all students the access to whatever they feel can educate/develop them
- Tailored support for all children, young people and families, regardless of gender, culture or disabilities
- Regardless of age, sex, needs, feeling that you are comfortable and having equal rights to equivalent opportunities
- Every child has the right to be in the setting where they feel they belong

(Continued)

(Continued)

- From each according to their ability to each according to their need
- Being used as a shorthand for being educated in a mainstream school
- Opportunities to mix with their peers in whatever activity/setting is most appropriate for them
- Providing the best opportunity for success for all in a setting that is best for each individual
- Each individual feels s/he is part of a class group and part of the whole school community
- What should be a positive experience … but is often square pegs in round holes
- Understanding and celebrating the unique qualities of each child and ensuring a sense of belonging.

Activity

1. Look through the descriptions of inclusion and pick out five or six that you think are closest to matching your own opinion.

    Write them on separate pieces of paper and place them in order with your favourite one at the top.

    Compare your findings with someone else who has done the same exercise.

    Discuss your reasons for which ones will make the final top six you decide on together.

2. Have a go separately, and then together, at seeing if there is a definition you prefer to any you have discussed so far. If you are satisfied that you cannot find a better definition, then decide which is your favourite and whether you both agree on the same one.

Both Newham and North Tyneside could be said to have a flexible range of provision, although the emphasis may be different. Over many years, Newham has put money into mainstream schools to provide them with the resources to cater for a very wide range of needs. North Tyneside has more special schools and has co-located some of its specialist teams with them. Both have a number of resourced provisions, which, with specialist and advisory teams, help to form a continuum of provision, giving choice to parents and moving away from segregated sectors.

'Different for different – an inclusive pedagogy.'

The development of SEN provision in New Zealand

In previous chapters, there have been references to what is happening in the rest of Europe. Looking further afield, this next section provides a snapshot of the development of SEN provision in New Zealand. In 1989, the country passed an Education Act giving disabled children the right to attend their local school. In 1993 it signed the 1990 United Nations Convention on the Rights of Children (UNCRC), which was discussed in the introductory chapter to this book. In 1995, policy guidelines from the government stated that special education is for those who require support or resources beyond that of the regular school. Soon after this, the government in New Zealand developed 'Special Education 2000', which was aimed at achieving a world-class inclusive system over the next decade. A Disability Strategy followed in 2001 which described how to provide the best education for disabled young people. In 2007 Autistic Spectrum Disorder Guidelines were issued, followed in 2010 by a Review of Special Education, which produced *Success for All: Every School, Every Child*. A survey at this time showed that 99% of respondents were in favour of retaining special schools, after which the government agreed that special schools would continue to be part of a continuum of provision.

Having settled the future of special schools, in 2015 an Update, rather than a Review, started. The aims of the Update are:

- To put achievement and participation at the heart of the support for children and young people
- To remove barriers at every stage of the education pathway
- To provide certainty for parents and whānau (the Māori word for families)
- To improve early identification of the need for additional support and early response.

Consideration is also being given to co-ordinating the support for SEN; improving access to services and decision-making for families; and reducing waiting times for support. Some of the ways that are being discussed to enable this to happen include: having a single point of contact for everyone involved in the education of a child with SEN; ensuring there is appropriate assessment of their progress and achievement; and ensuring co-ordination between education, health and welfare systems.

Schools in New Zealand

Compulsory education is from 6 to 16 years of age, although most children start at 5. There are three main types of schools:

- State schools – attended by most of the population
- State integrated schools – either faith schools or ones following particular pedagogies such as Steiner or Montessori, which roughly 10% of the population attend
- Private schools, which cater for around 5% of the population.

There is a variable pattern of provision, so some children will stay in primary school until they are 12, while others will move to an intermediate school for 11- and 12-year-olds. Secondary schools are called grammar schools, high schools or colleges. All students have to learn about Māori culture and language as part of the curriculum.

Specialist provision

There are 28 day special schools and residential special schools for hearing impairment, visual impairment, and severe behaviour, social or emotional needs with underlying cognitive impairment. There are also centres for children and young people with sensory impairments. Most special schools have satellites in mainstream schools, where the classes are managed and staffed by the special school. Apart from the residential special schools, the others are generic because the population does not allow for the different types of special schools that are common in the UK. Most also operate outreach services. Graeme Daniel is the President of the Special Education Principals' Association of New Zealand (SEPAnz), which was formed in 1989 to be the national voice for special schools and their communities. Its slogan reads: 'It's not where, it's how'.

Graeme's own school is Allenvale School in Christchurch. He has seen a similar rise in pupils on the autism spectrum and with SLD and PMLD. Twelve per cent of his population are Māori children and there is concern throughout the country that their progress and achievement are not as high as they are for non-Māori students. Māori children generally prefer not to be taught as individuals, but are likely to be more engaged in learning when taught as a group. The school's uniforms are designed using fabrics that assist students with sensory issues. As Graeme says, they won't learn unless they are comfortable. His school is due to become the first co-located school in the country, with others to follow. Although there are those who are not comfortable with specialist provision (whom he refers to as 'inclusion protagonists'), as he points out, 'Not all children flourish in the same environment'.

In this brief glimpse of another country and its search for the best way of educating all children, it is interesting to note the parallels with the UK. In New Zealand, this has seen a move from an uncertain future for special schools to embedding them as part of the network of provision, including special schools having satellite classes in mainstream schools and providing specialist teacher outreach services, hence the move to a dual role. The move to having co-located mainstream and special schools will help to ensure that there is a more seamless continuum of provision.

An overview of inclusion

Throughout this book, a case has been made for interpreting inclusion as a process rather than a place and for having a continuum of provision which enables all young learners (and their educational establishments) to feel included. Terms like 'segregated provision' are no longer seen as relevant as schools and other settings are working together to provide a continuum of provision for pupils with SEND and other vulnerable groups. Furthermore, all types of provision are being used more flexibly, with a growing number of co-located schools and other settings offering part-time, short-term or dual-roll placements for pupils where this is appropriate. It is no longer the case that special schools are isolated along with the pupils who attend them. Most have formal or less formal arrangements for offering outreach and consultancy services to colleagues, fulfilling with enthusiasm the idea of having a dual role. The growth in the population of pupils with very complex needs has created a demand for more specialist provision in all its forms.

There have been concerns expressed in some quarters that it is only by closing special schools that mainstream schools will take seriously the need to become more skilled. Yet, it has been shown that mainstream schools have welcomed many pupils who might formerly have been in special schools and adapted their ways of working to accommodate them. There is also a need to have centres of expertise, through specialist support services, through resourced mainstream provisions and through special schools, so that they can provide the training and support that is required. The final chapter will take up some of these themes by discussing what else needs to happen to make sure children, young people and their families receive the support they deserve.

'Accept them as they are and not against some expected norms.'

Summary

This chapter has covered developments in the local authorities of Newham and North Tyneside. Some conclusions were drawn about how, in different ways, they have arrived at a pattern of provision that fits in with their areas. Both represent a continuum of opportunities for children and young people with SEND and a degree of choice for their families.

This was followed by a consideration of how New Zealand is developing its specialist provision and comparisons were drawn with the

(Continued)

(Continued)

UK. Although special schools in New Zealand are more generic due to their scattered populations, there are more similarities than differences in the way the countries have developed their specialist provision.

The chapter ended with some comments on the need to agree on a wider definition of inclusion than one that refers to full inclusion in mainstream provision, so that the debate can be put to bed and there is a consensus about how to move forward together.

Further reading

Burnett, N. (2005) *Leadership and SEN: Meeting the Challenge in Special and Mainstream Settings.* London: David Fulton.

Carpenter, B. et al. (2015) *Engaging Learners with Complex Learning Difficulties and Disabilities: A Resource Book for Teachers and Teaching Assistants.* London: Routledge.

Crossley-Holland, J. (2013) *The Future Role of the Local Authority in Education.* http://adcs.org.uk/assets/documentation/Future_role_of_the_local_authority_in_school_improvement_report.pdf

Tutt, R. and Williams, P. (2012) *How Successful Schools Work: The Impact of Innovative Leadership.* London: Sage.

7

Conclusions: A system fit for the 21st century

'Inclusion is a process not a place.'

The opening chapter of this book showed that, although attitudes towards people who are disabled or have special educational needs have changed dramatically, from trying to hide them away to wanting to include them, there is still a misconception about the meaning of inclusion. Difficulties have arisen when the concept of inclusion has been interpreted too narrowly and taken to mean that every child or young person should be educated in a mainstream setting. This simplistic view leads to little attention being paid to whether a child's needs could actually be met in a mainstream classroom, or, indeed, whether the child could cope with being in a setting geared to the needs of the majority. This could be said to be an attitude that puts a principle before the needs of the individual. Inevitably, it also reduces parental choice.

Inclusion being referred to as a place rather than a process resulted in the denigration of special schools during the 1980s and 1990s, when parents and carers were made to feel that, however complex their child's needs, mainstream education was not only the best place for them, but that they had a right to be there. This meant that special schools went from being seen as the civilised and effective way of educating pupils with the most complex needs, to being under threat of survival. It was not until the turn of the century that a more realistic view began to emerge, which resulted in special schools having the opportunity to move from being seen as segregated provision to becoming embedded in the school system as a whole.

Throughout this book, there have been case studies of former barriers being broken down, as co-located schools, multi-academy trusts (MATs), teaching school alliances and various other formal and informal partnerships, have seen schools working together to the benefit of all pupils, including those who have special educational needs and disabilities (SEND) and other vulnerable groups. In fact, it is heart-warming what has been achieved when there remains some confusion about inclusion. Although it was the report of the Warnock Committee that started the debate, Warnock herself has made it clear, for example in the pamphlet she wrote in 2005, that inclusion should be interpreted as 'including all children in the common educational enterprise of learning, wherever they learn best'. While accepting that the vast majority of pupils with SEND will be, as they should be and always have been, in mainstream schools, she has been particularly concerned to recognise young learners who do not feel comfortable in a large, complex, and for them, confusing environment.

While the flow between former sectors is increasing all the time, it would have moved faster if a common understanding of inclusion had been there. All too often, the word is still used as a shorthand for meaning 'inclusion in a mainstream school'. Yet, if questioned, most people will say that they do not believe all pupils should be educated in their local school, regardless of the complexity of the needs, the resources within the school to meet those needs, or their own wishes (where they are able to express them) and those of their family. Indeed, there is a general recognition at all levels that, for a variety of reasons, not least the significant rise of a more complex population, there is a greater need than ever for a range of specialist and alternative provision.

Although schools and services have been able to get on with creating a continuum of provision, the lack of certainty about where inclusion is going has meant that provision has developed in different ways according to the views of those involved at national and local level, rather than having a common understanding that everyone is marching in step towards a common goal. The likelihood of qualifying for an Education, Health and Care plan (EHC plan), which, for some, will be the first step towards a specialist placement, may depend as much on where someone lives as on the severity of the child's needs. How much better it would be if politicians of all parties climbed off the fence and produced a clear statement about inclusion being a process not a place and that all types of specialist provision, including special schools, would continue to be valued as part of a flexible continuum of provision.

Instead, for decades there has been a series of contradictory statements, when, unusually for political parties, there is actually much agreement between them about inclusion. Indeed, it was a Labour government who first talked about inclusion being a process and who set up a working party to look at the future of special schooling. This fed into its SEN strategy,

Removing Barriers to Achievement (DfES, 2004a). Yet, when the Education Select Committee (2005–06) pointed out that the strategy said that numbers in special schools were expected to decline, the answer was that they did not mind if numbers stabilised around the figure at the time. The Conservatives, who have generally been seen as more supportive of special schools, said in their 2010 Manifesto that: 'The most vulnerable children deserve the very highest quality of care, so we will call a moratorium on the ideologically-driven closure of special schools. We will end the bias towards the inclusion of children with special needs in mainstream schools'. And, here, it was made quite plain that it was inclusion *in mainstream schools* that was meant. However, the phrase 'the bias towards inclusion' was later removed and replaced in the Children and Families Act (2014) with the current phrase about 'the presumption of mainstream schooling', while still stressing that parents must have an equal right to choose a mainstream or a special school for their child.

It is as if everyone wants to pussyfoot around the subject in the hope that no one will be upset by what they say. Yet, in fact, a large majority of people want to see a range of provision and this has been confirmed by parents having to go to the SEND Tribunal to get their children *into* special schools, whereas the fight used to be all the other way. Despite the contradictions and lack of clarity, schools have moved a long way since an Ofsted report in 2006, *Inclusion: Does it Matter where Pupils are Taught?*, noted a gulf between mainstream and special schools with comments such as: 'Mainstream and special schools continued to struggle to establish an equal partnership. Good collaboration was rare'. Today, it would be hard to find examples of schools that were not collaborating in this way, as illustrated by the case studies in this book, and the very many other examples that there was not room to include.

'They need to feel OK about themselves or their life chances are damaged.'

The quote that follows is from a profoundly deaf adult who is looking back on his childhood. He is now pursuing a career as a design engineer. He says:

> I am aware that I was one of the lucky ones to live near a deaf school providing accessible education methods using total communication. I believe fluent signing teachers of the deaf present in schools to interact with deaf children will help enormously for them to access information through a language that is accessible to every child, as every child can learn how to sign but not every child can learn to speak.

Another contribution is from a young lady who also looks back with affection on her time at a special school. She says:

Special school helped me to learn the skills needed in order to thrive as an individual. It was like a family unit where you met different people in different situations. It was fun too and loads of happy memories were had. I even had a stint working there as a midday supervisory assistant (MSA) as an adult and enjoyed being back and the children were interested in my previous experience and asked me lots of questions of being in their school as a child.

Of course, it would be possible to find plenty of examples of people who had either enjoyed or hated their schooling, whether it was mainstream or special, but the examples are mentioned because each gives an insight into the pupil's experience. A head teacher who had worked in several mainstream and special schools, when talking about raising pupils' self-esteem, put it like this:

This is something that special schools are really good at. It's harder in mainstream, which is fine for the majority with SEN, but a minority need a different setting. I didn't realise this until I moved from mainstream to special. Now, pupils who come to us, particularly if they arrive late, it becomes much clearer. Some are clinically depressed and even then, they manage to recover because of the impact of this environment.

Considerable progress has been made, perhaps in spite of, rather than because of, any clear direction from the top. Up to a point, this has been useful in proving that schools, services and settings are keen to work together and realise the value of doing so, particularly in the case of children and young people who have SEND or are vulnerable for other reasons, such as being in care, or are themselves young carers; having disorganised home lives, disrupted schooling, or suffering from deprivation. On the other hand, a properly planned and joined-up continuum of provision has been slower to emerge. And this has led to an even slower take-up of seeing how it could be used more flexibly to meet the needs of a wider group of children, offer earlier intervention and provide for children's different and changing needs.

The closing paragraphs of this book are concerned with how to move forward from here and build on the work that has already been achieved. Below, some steps to the way forward are suggested:

1 A common understanding of inclusion

First, there needs to be an end to using the word 'inclusion' as a shorthand way of saying that every child should be educated in a mainstream school. This is done so frequently that people often do not stop to think, and when challenged, will generally say that that is not what they mean.

2 Inclusion as a process

Second, it needs to be recognised that any school or setting, whether mainstream or special, academy or maintained, specialist or alternative provision, is capable of being inclusive or not being inclusive. The Inclusion Quality Mark (IQM) has shown this to be the case, which has helped people to be more aware of what inclusion entails.

3 A continuum of provision

Third, every LA should make sure that there is a continuum of provision in their area, from support in mainstream classes for the majority of pupils with SEND at one end, to a 24-hour curriculum in 52-week provision at the other, and with every variation in between.

4 Using the continuum flexibly for SEND pupils

Fourth, once this common understanding is in place, there should be far greater scope to use the provision that exists in a much more flexible manner. It is happening now, but it is happening patchily. One of the reasons why it is not happening more widely is because special schools and some other specialist settings are rarely allowed to take in pupils without statements or EHC plans. There is now the possibility of some special academies being able to do this, but this needs to be extended more widely so that more children can benefit.

'I want to show you what I can do, not what I can't.'

Assessment placements

There needs to be a far greater recognition of the value of assessment placements to find out what a child can or cannot do in a school context, rather than relying on how they perform in a short time with a professional they may not know. (This is not instead of the appropriate professionals being involved, but in addition to, for example, an educational psychologist's (EP) report, the input from a speech and language therapist (SaLT), or the involvement of a teacher of the deaf).

Short-term provision

In addition to assessment placements which are short-term, there needs to be the flexibility for pupils, with or without EHC plans, to benefit from a short time in a specialist setting. Some time ago there were examples of short-term provision being available, but when statements came in, this largely disappeared. Short-term provision should be available for any pupil with SEND who needs it, whether or not they have a statement or EHC plan. Children's circumstances change, they have illnesses, or they may simply be falling behind, but with full-time specialist help, many will catch up before the gap gets too large and goes on growing. Specialist provision, whether in mainstream or special schools, is expensive, but this is a way of maximising its use, and, in the longer term, it is cost-effective.

Part-time provision

These are often informal arrangements between schools put in place for a number of reasons, such as pupils benefitting from being on the roll of one school, but having the opportunity to take part in lessons or activities in another school. This may be a longer-term arrangement, or, for instance, the start of a move into a special school or a move back to mainstream.

Dual roll

This is usually the result of an agreement between a combination of a mainstream school, a special school, a pupil referral unit (PRU) or alternative provision (AP), that the best way of meeting a pupil's needs is to split their time between two provisions and for them to be on the roll of more than one school. Again, this opens up another way of meeting pupils' different needs.

Individual packages of support

As schools of all kinds become more inclusive and flexible in their approach, it becomes easier to think outside the normal boundaries of what usually happens in schools, which, by their very nature, are class based, and to offer an individual package of support to a pupil, if that is the best way of meeting their needs. To some extent, education has become more personalised for all pupils and the value of building on their strengths and interests has been recognised and responded to. For a few more vulnerable individuals, it may be a question of meeting them more than halfway in order to address their very individual needs and to motivate or enable them to learn.

Bespoke services

At one extreme of the SEND continuum are the young people who need both education and residential provision all the year round, as a way of putting together their fractured lives. This is another type of provision that seems very expensive, but not if, in the longer term, it enables people to lead fulfilled and productive lives.

5 The need for more specialist provision not less

Another reason why special schools should no longer have to fear for their future is the rising population of children and young people who have very complex needs and, in some cases, are different to pupils with SEND in the past. This creates a greater need for specialist placements of all kinds, including in special schools and resourced mainstream schools, and for the expertise of specialist support services. As a result, many special schools are under a different kind of pressure; not wondering if they will be closed, but how they are going to fit in the pupils queuing at their doors. As this situation is not likely to go away within the foreseeable future, it makes sense to stop thinking in terms of full inclusion of all pupils in mainstream schools and to start talking about how special schools can become centres of expertise, where the best equipment and the most effective approaches are based on the findings of teacher-led research working alongside neuroscientists and other researchers in universities.

> *'Staff must want to learn and to grow – that's how schools become outstanding.'*

6 Creating a continuum of expertise

This leads into the sixth strand, firstly to join up the expertise that is already there and, secondly, to put in place the means to have a supply of staff who have the skills and training to meet children and young people's diverse needs. There are some interesting examples in this book and elsewhere of specialist support services working together with special schools or other forms of specialist provision, to co-ordinate and extend the available expertise. A dual role for special schools is seen within this context. At a time when money is tight and SEN Support Services may be under threat, it becomes even more important to ensure that everyone is working together. A further extension is the need for professionals from across the services of education, health and social care to train and work together, enhancing the skill set of all those involved. Again, there have been some case studies of where this is happening, but there is a long way to go. There is a dearth of joint training opportunities and these need to become much more common, from conferences to qualifications that go across health, social care and education, in various combinations.

As far as those in education are concerned, where significant and obvious steps need to be taken is in initial teacher training (ITT) and continuing professional development (CPD). Currently, there is a review of how to ensure all trainee teachers have a better understanding of SEND. But, beyond this, there needs to be a similar model to the one featured in *Removing Barriers to Achievement* (DfES, 2004a), but never fully implemented.

In addition, there is a need for a general pathway and more specific training (see Figure 7.1). The amount that is available, either face to face, online or through blended learning, is quite exciting. What is needed now is to co-ordinate it, so that there are clearly defined pathways to becoming better informed about different aspects of SEND. At national level, it would be possible to plot what is already there and then to think in terms of how to fill in the gaps.

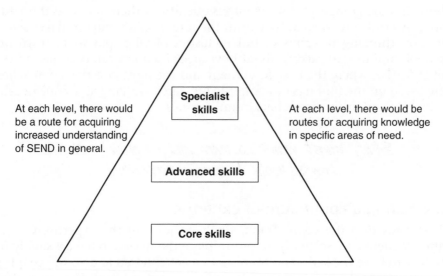

Figure 7.1   Levels of training

Source: Adapted from *Removing Barriers to Achievement*, DfES 2004a, para 3.9.

Final thoughts

There are different ways of looking at the current climate for SEND. One is to become disheartened by the clash of agendas whereby successive gov-ernments have imposed accountability measures on schools that value attainment over achievement and threaten the self-esteem of any pupil who happens not to be of average and above ability (or, if they are, their difficulties prevent them from showing it). On the other hand, it is possi-ble to marvel at the dogged determination of those working in the field, who do what they can to ignore the arguments and the lack of a coherent message and simply get on with trying to discover what works best for each individual. These are the people who treat every day, every lesson and every activity as an opportunity to engage the reluctant or recalcitrant learner and to enthuse and encourage those for whom learning may seem to be a constant battle. They are the ones who, despite the demands and the difficulties of the job, find time to remember that the withdrawn child who sits in silent despair and the one who is disrupting their lesson may be equally unhappy with how they are and equally in need of support and understanding.

David Bateson, who chairs the National SEND Forum (NSENDF) and has spent a lifetime learning about what works for pupils with SEND, puts it like this: 'Inclusion is a state of being, not a place. It's the flexibility that brings about the right provision at the right time in the right place with the right people'.

What is beyond doubt is that there is a growing continuum of provision, that special schools after years of isolation are thoroughly embedded in the school system and that the more people find ways of working together across schools, across services and with parents and families, the more likely it is that answers will be found as to how to reach and teach every child and young person, no matter how complex their needs.

'Help them to grow from where they are, not from where someone else thinks they should be.'

Useful websites

Education

Achievement for All (AfA)	www.afaeducation.org
Anti-Bullying Alliance	www.anti-bullyingalliance.org.uk
Enterprise Education	www.enterprise-education.org.uk
Equals	www.equals.co.uk
Inclusion Quality Mark	www.inclusionmark.co.uk
nasen	www.nasen.org.uk
New Schools Network (NSN)	www.newschoolsnetwork.org
The Nurture Group Network	www.nurturegroups.org; www.boxallprofile.org
PRUsAP	www.prusap.org.uk
ResearchED	www.workingoutwhatworks.com
Association of National Specialist Colleges (Natspec)	www.natspec.org.uk

Mental health

Body Gossip	www.bodygossip.org
British Association of Counselling and Psychotherapists (BACP)	www.bacp.co.uk
The Self-Esteem Team	www.selfesteemteam.org
Strengths & Difficulties Questionnaire (SDQ)	www.sdqinfo.com
Young Minds	www.youngminds.org.uk

Organisations for different needs

All-Party Parliamentary Group on FASD	www.appg-fasd.org.uk
National Organisation for Foetal Alcohol Syndrome – UK	www.nofas-uk.org
The Fragile X Society UK	www.fragilex.org.uk

National Deaf Children's Society (NDCS)	www.ndcs.org.uk
PDA Society	www.pdasociety.org.uk
Royal National Institute of Blind People (RNIB)	www.rnib.org.uk
Scope (formerly Spastics Society)	www.scope.org.uk
Sense (deafblind people/MSI)	www.sense.org.uk

Resources

Assessing Intellectual and Reasoning Skills	www.frankwise.oxon.sch.uk; www.tes.com/teaching-resources
Autism Education Trust (AET)	www.autismeducationtrust.org.uk
The Communication Trust	www.thecommunicationtrust.org.uk
The Dyslexia–SpLD Trust	www.thedyslexia-spldtrust.org.uk
Complex Needs materials	www.complexneeds.org.uk
The Lamb materials	www.advanced-training.org.uk
nasen's SEND Gateway	www.sendgateway.org.uk

Support for families

Bliss	www.bliss.org.uk
Contact a Family	www.caf.org.uk
4Children	www.4children.org.uk
Independent Parental Special Education Advice (IPSEA)	www.ipsea.org.uk
Kids Children's Charity	www.kids.org.uk
National Network of Parent Carer Forums	www.nnpcf.org.uk
Local Parent Carer Forums (contact through the National Network of Parent Carer Forums)	
Special Needs Jungle	www.specialneedsjungle.com
The Who Cares? Trust	www.thewhocarestrust.org.uk
Unique	www.rarechromo.org
Wraparound Partnership	www.wraparoundpartnership.org

Therapies

Creative therapies	www.creativetherapies.co.uk
Rebound therapy	www.reboundtherapy.org
Thrive	www.thriveapproach.co.uk

References and further reading

All-Party Parliamentary Group (APPG) for FASD (2015) *Initial Report of the Inquiry into the Current Picture of FASD in the UK Today.* www.appg-fasd.org.uk

Bennett, T. (2015) *Managing Difficult Behaviour in Schools: A Practical Guide.* London: Unison. https://www.unison.org.uk/content/uploads/2015/04/On-line-Catalogue 22970.pdf

Board of Education (1918) *Education Act.* London: HMSO.

Board of Education (1944) *Education Act.* London: HMSO.

Burnett, N. (2005) *Leadership and SEN: Meeting the Challenge in Special and Mainstream Settings.* London: David Fulton.

Carpenter, B. et al. (2015) *Engaging Learners with Complex Learning Difficulties and Disabilities: A Resource Book for Teachers and Teaching Assistants.* Abingdon: Routledge.

Cheminais, R. (2015) *Rita Cheminais' Handbook for SENCOs.* London: Sage.

Crossley-Holland, J. (2013) *The Future Role of the Local Authority in Education.* http://adcs.org.uk/assets/documentation/Future_role_of_the_local_authority_in_school_improvement_report.pdf

DCSF (2009) *Lamb Inquiry: Special Educational Needs and Parental Confidence.* http://webarchive.nationalarchives.gov.uk/20130401151715/https://www.education.gov.uk/publications/standard/publicationdetail/page1/dcsf-01143-2009

DENI (2015) *Review of Special School Provision in Northern Ireland.* https://www.deni.gov.uk/publications/review-special-school-provision-northern-ireland

DES (1970) *Education (Handicapped Children) Act.* London: HMSO.

DES (1978) *The Warnock Report: Special Educational Needs – Report of the Committee of Enquiry into the Education of Handicapped Children and Young People.* London: HMSO.

DES (1981) *Education Act.* London: HMSO

DES (1988) *Education Reform Act.* London: HMSO.

DfE (1994) *Code of Practice on the Identification and Assessment of Special Education Needs.* London: HMSO.

DfE (2010a) *Equality Act.* London: HMSO.

DfE (2010b) *Green Paper: Children and Young People with Special Educational Needs and Disabilities – Call for Views.* London: HMSO.

DfE (2011) *Support and Aspiration: A New Approach to Special Educational Needs and Disability – a Consultation.* http://webarchive.nationalarchives.gov.uk/20130401151715/https://www.education.gov.uk/publications/eorderingdownload/green-paper-sen.pdf

DfE (2014a) *Children and Families Act.* www.legislation.gov.uk/ukpga/2014/6/contents/enacted

DfE (2014b) *Supported Internships: Advice for FE Colleges, Sixth Forms in Academies, Maintained and Non-maintained Schools, Independent Specialist Providers, Other Providers of Study Programmes and Local Authorities.* https://www.gov.uk/government/uploads/system/uploads/attachment_data/file/389411/Supported_Internship_Guidance_Dec_14.pdf

DfE (2014c) *Preventing and Tackling Bullying – Advice for headteachers, staff and governing bodies*. www.gov.uk/government/uploads/system/uploads/attachment_data/file/444862/Preventing_and_tackling_bullying_advice.pdf

DfE (2015a) *Special Educational Needs and Disability Code of Practice: 0–25 Years*. https://www.gov.uk/government/uploads/system/uploads/attachment_data/file/398815/SEND_Code_of_Practice_January_2015.pdf

DfE (2015b) *Counselling in Schools: A Blueprint for the Future – Departmental Advice for School Leaders and Counsellors*. https://www.gov.uk/government/publications/counselling-in-schools

DfE (2015c) *A Guide to Exclusions Statistics July 2015*. www.gov.uk/government/publications

DfE (2015d) *Carter Review of Initial Teacher Training (ITT)*. https://www.gov.uk/government/uploads/system/uploads/attachment_data/file/399957/Carter_Review.pdf

DfE (2015e) *Government Response to the Carter Review of Initial Teacher Training (ITT)*. https://www.gov.uk/government/uploads/system/uploads/attachment_data/file/396461/Carter_Review_Government_response_20150119.pdf

DfE (2015f) *Mental Health and Behaviour in Schools: Departmental Advice for School Staff*. https://www.gov.uk/government/publications/mental-health-and-behaviour-in-schools–2

DfE (2015g) *Commission on Assessment Without Levels: Final Report*. https://www.gov.uk/government/publications/commission-on-assessment-without-levels-final-report

DfE (2015h) *Statement on the Interim Recommendations of the Rochford Review*. www.gov.uk/government/uploads/system/uploads_data/file/498204/Interim_recommendations_of_the_Rockford_Review.pdf

DfE (2015i) *Special Educational Needs Survey 2016 – Guide to the completion of the SEN2 return, version 1.3*. www.gov.uk/government/publications/special-educational-needs-survey-2016-guide

DfE (2015j) *Measuring the Performance of Schools within Academy Chains and Local Authorities – A Statistical Working Paper*. www.gov.uk/government/uploads/system/uploads/attachment-data/file/415659/SFR09-2015.pdf

DfE (2015k) *Statement on the Interim Recommendations of the Rochford Review*. https://www.gov.uk/.../rochford-review-interim-recommendations

DfE (2015l) *Pre-key Stage 1: Pupils Working below the Test Standard*. www.gov.uk/government/publications/pre-key-stage-1-pupils-working-below-the-test-standard

DfE (2015m) *Pre-key Stage 2: Pupils Working below the Test Standard*. www.gov.uk/government/publications/pre-key-stage-1-pupils-working-below-the-test-standard

DfE (2016a) *White Paper: Educational Excellence Everywhere*. www.gov.uk/government/publications

DfE (2016b) *Education and Adoption Act*. Norwich: TSO.

DfE (2016c) *Mental Health and Behaviour in Schools: Departmental Advice for School Staff*. www.gov.uk/government/.../mental-health-and-behaviour-in-schools-2

DfES (2001a) *Special Educational Needs and Disability Act*. Nottingham: DfES Publications.

DFES (2001b) *Special Educational Needs: Code of Practice*. Nottingham: DfES Publications.

DfES (2004a) *Removing Barriers to Achievement: The Government's Strategy for SEN*. Nottingham: DfES Publications.

DfES (2004b) *Children Act*. Nottingham: DfES Publications.

Dittrich, W.H. and Tutt, R. (2008) *Educating Children with Complex Conditions: Understanding Overlapping and Co-existing Developmental Disorders*. London: Sage.

DoH & NHS England (2015) *Future in Mind: Promoting, Protecting and Improving Children and Young People's Mental Health and Wellbeing*. https://www.gov.uk/government/uploads/system/uploads/attachment_data/file/414024/Childrens_Mental_Health.pdf

Driver Youth Trust (2015) *Joining the Dots: Have the Recent Reforms Worked for Those with SEND?* www.driveryouthtrust.com

Foxwell, L. and Tutt, R. *(2014) A Practical Guide to Supporting EAL and SEN Learners*. Kingsteignton: LS Books.

Greig, G. (2011) *The King Maker: The Man Who Saved George VI*. London: Hodder and Stoughton.

Hicks, A. (2015) *Matters of the Mind: Speaking Out About Mental Health in Schools*. http://www.huffingtonpost.co.uk/anna-hicks/mental-health_b_7268330.html

Hodkinson, A. (2015) *Key Issues in Special Educational Needs and Inclusion*, 2nd edition. London: Sage.

House of Commons Education and Skills Committee (2005–6) *Special Educational Needs: Third Report of Session 2005–06*. London: HMSO.

Kirby, A. (2013) *How to Succeed in College and University with Specific Learning Difficulties: A Guide for Students, Educators & Parents*. London: Souvenir Press.

Larkey, S. (2006) *Practical Sensory Programmes for Students with ASD and Other Special Needs*. London: Jessica Kingsley.

Martin, V. and students of Limpsfield Grange (2015) *M is for Autism*. London: Jessica Kingsley.

Meijer, C. (2010) 'Special Needs Education in Europe: Inclusive Policies and Practices', *Zeitschrift für inclusion*, 2010: 2. www.inklusion-online.net/index.php/inklusion-online/article/view/136/136

Ministry of New Zealand (1989) *Education Act*. http://www.legislation.govt.nz/act/public/1989/0080/latest/whole.html

Ministry of New Zealand (2010) *Success for All: Every School, Every Child*. http://www.education.govt.nz/assets/Documents/School/Inclusive-education/SuccessForAllEnglish.pdf

NCTL (2014) *Impact of Teaching Schools*. https://www.gov.uk/government/uploads/system/uploads/attachment_data/file/309938/teaching-schools-impact-report-2014.pdf

Norwich, B. (2013) *Addressing Tensions and Dilemmas in Inclusive Education: Living with Uncertainty*. London: Routledge.

Ofsted (2006) *Inclusion: Does it Matter Where Children Are Taught?* www.education.gov.uk/publications/.../HMI-2535.doc.doc

Ofsted (2010) *The Special Educational Needs and Disability Review: A Statement is Not Enough*. https://www.gov.uk/government/uploads/system/uploads/attachment_data/file/413814/Special_education_needs_and_disability_review.pdf

Ofsted (2014) *Inspecting Extended School Provision*. www.ofsted.gov.uk/resources/100145

Peacey, N. (2015) 'A Transformation or an Opportunity Lost?' A discussion paper prepared for Research and Information on State Education (RISE). www.risetrust.org.uk

PSHE Association (2015) *Teacher Guidance: Preparing to Teach about Mental Health and Emotional Wellbeing*. https://www.pshe-association.org.uk/curriculum-and-resources/resources/guidance-preparing-teach-about-mental-health-and-emotional-wellbeing

Rayner, S. (2007) *Managing Special and Inclusive Education*. London: Sage.

Rees Centre (2015) *The Educational Progress of Looked After Children in England: Linking Care and Educational Data*. http://reescentre.education.ox.ac.uk/research/ educational-progress-of-looked-after-children/

Shakespeare, T. and Watson, N. (2002) 'The Social Model of Disability: An Outdated Ideology?' *Research in Social Science and Disability*, 2: 9–28.

Stanley, E. (2015) 'Power to Parents', *SEN Magazine*, November. www.senmagazine. co.uk

Stobbs, P. (2012) 'Overview of Previous National SEND Achievements and their Fit with Current SEND Policy Directions', *The Coalition Government's Policy on SEND: Aspirations and Challenges?* Policy Paper, SEN Policy Research Forum. www. sen-policyforum.org.uk

Sutton Trust (2015) *CHAIN EFFECTS 2015 – The Impact of Academy Chains on Low Income Students*. www.suttontrust.com

Tavassoli, T. and Brand, A. (2011) *Sensory Processing in Autism and the Built Environment*. Autism Research Centre, University of Cambridge and Royal College of Art, Helen Hamlyn Centre, NAS.

The Scottish Government (2004) *The Education (Additional Support for Learning) (Scotland) Act*. www.gov.scot/Publications

Tutt, R. (2007) *Every Child Included*. London: Sage.

Tutt, R. (2011) *Partnership Working to Support Special Educational Needs and Disabilities*. London: Sage.

Tutt, R. and Williams, P. (2014) *How Successful Schools Work: The Impact of Innovative School Leadership*. London: Sage.

Tutt, R. and Williams, P. (2015) *The SEND Code of Practice 0–25 Years: Policy, Provision and Practice*. London: Sage.

UN (2006) *UN Convention on the Rights of Persons with Disabilities* (UNCRPD). http:// www.un.org/disabilities/convention/conventionfull.shtml

Unesco (1994) *The Salamanca Statement and Framework for Action*. www.unesco.org/ education/pdf /SALAMA.EPDF

Unicef (1989) *UN Convention on the Rights of the Child* (UNCRC). www.unicef. org/crc/

Warnock, M. (1978) *Report of the Committee of Enquiry into the Education of Handicapped Children and Young People*. London: HMSO.

Warnock, M. (2005) *Special Educational Needs: A New Look*, Paper 11. London: Philosophy of Education Society of Great Britain.

Welsh Government (2015) *Draft Additional Learning Needs Bill – Wales*. www.gov. wales/consultations/.../draft-aln-and-education

Index